T0123290

I TOLD YOU SO

I TOLD YOU SO

I TOLD YOU SO
Gore Vidal
Talks Politics

Interviews with Jon Wiener

COUNTERPOINT
BERKELEY

I Told You So: Gore Vidal Talks Politics
Interviews with Jon Wiener
This collection © 2012 Jon Wiener

First published in the United States by OR Books New York, 2012.

All rights reserved under International and Pan-American Copyright
Conventions. No part of this book may be used or reproduced in any
manner whatsoever without written permission from the publisher, except
in the case of brief quotations embodied in critical articles and reviews.

Permissions included on page 143

Library of Congress Cataloging-in-Publication is available
ISBN 978-1-61902-174-7

COUNTERPOINT
2560 Ninth Street, Suite 318
Berkeley, CA 94710
www.counterpointpress.com

" The four most beautiful words in our common language:

I told you so."

—Gore Vidal

CONTENTS

INTRODUCTION Gore Vidal as a Talker   9

1 Los Angeles Times Festival of Books   13
   Royce Hall, UCLA
   April 28, 2007

2 Los Angeles Institute for the Humanities   27
   University of Southern California
   December 15, 2006

3 The 2000 Shadow Convention Radio Interview   47
   Plaza Hotel, New York City
   September 9, 2000

4 *Radical History Review* Interview   83
   Ravello, Italy
   July 12, 1988

   POSTSCRIPT Remembering Gore Vidal   127

   ACKNOWLEDGMENTS   133

   NOTES   135

Gore Vidal in conversation with Jon Wiener at the *Los Angeles Times* Festival of Books, April 28, 2007.

INTRODUCTION
Gore Vidal as a Talker

Gore Vidal was a great talker as well as a great writer. Dick Cavett called him "the best talker since Oscar Wilde." He talked a lot; if you Google "Gore Vidal interview," you get 40,000 results. But what remains of those is mostly one-liners, quips and zingers, about Truman Capote, William F. Buckley and George Bush. This book offers Vidal in a more sustained mode of conversation: developing arguments, tracing connections between past and present, citing evidence. Of course he provides plenty of one-liners and zingers along the way.

The four interviews here represent Gore talking about politics with me for different audiences: first, 2,000 enthusiastic fans at a book festival in Los Angeles; then sixty academics and writers at the Los Angeles Institute for the Humanities; then listeners at a left wing radio station in L.A.; and finally readers of the *Radical History Review*. These interviews cover a twenty-year span when he was at his best: we did the first in 1988 and the last in 2007. They are presented in reverse chronological order, with the most recent first.

The 1988 *Radical History Review* (*RHR*) interview was where I first met Gore. It's the most obscure—although after publication in the *RHR* it was excerpted in *Harper's* "Readings" and in a collection of Vidal interviews. He may have been willing to do this one because he had a long-standing critique of the mainstream of the history profession and I think welcomed the chance to speak to younger "radical" historians who were sympathetic to his left-wing vision of the American past. And although the *RHR* had a tiny readership, it had been running a series of interviews that were significant and prestigious; Pantheon had already published a collection that included the *RHR* interviews with E. P. Thompson, Eric Hobsbawm, William Appleman Williams, and others with whom Vidal was no doubt familiar.

In all our interviews I think he appreciated the opportunity talk seriously about things he really did care about: the history of the American Empire, the rise of the National Security State, and of course his own life in politics, as a commentator and as a candidate.

Since I asked the questions, I got to bring up things I was interested in. Often we started with things that were going on at the time we spoke, and then moved back to American politics and history earlier in the 20th century. Thus in 1988 I asked him about his novel *Empire*, which had just been published; in the fall of 2000, Al Gore and George W. Bush were running for president, and so was Ralph Nader, and Vidal's play *The Best Man* was being revived on Broadway, so we talked about those; and so on.

All four interviews have been condensed and edited. I have tried to eliminate repetition in Vidal's answers, but not always in the questions, because one of the interesting things here is to see how Gore answered the same question differently for different audiences. For example, the question "What gets you up in the morning? What keeps you going?": at the Book Festival in Los Angeles, with an audience of 2,000 fans, he answered "Rage." At the Humanities Institute in Los Angeles, with an audience of sixty intellectuals and writers, he answered "Stupidity." When asked who was the worst president, at the Book Festival he said "Bush;" at the Humanities Institute he said "Wilson"—and explained why.

And sometimes Vidal would direct his answer away from my question, and return to a topic that was important to him. Thus he always talked about his grandfather, the blind senator from Oklahoma; about the "rough treatment" he had received from the *New York Times* book reviewers; his views of how FDR got us into WWII; and of course the American Empire and the National Security State—so these repetitions remain as evidence of his passions and interests.

One thing is missing in these transcriptions: Vidal's speaking voice. It was marvelous, and unmistakable. He did uncanny imitations of JFK, Nixon, Eleanor Roosevelt, FDR, and of course he did a devastating Truman Capote. None of that is here, alas.

Headnotes to each interview sketch out the particular settings and circumstances.

—*Jon Wiener, Los Angeles, September 2012*

The Los Angeles Times *Festival of Books is a huge and wonderful annual event. More than 100,000 came to the UCLA campus in 2007, and one of the biggest attractions was Gore Vidal. He appeared onstage in the biggest theater on campus, historic Royce Hall, with 2,000 seats. The event had been sold out almost as soon as tickets became available, and the standby line went around the building.*

Six months earlier his memoir Point to Point Navigation *had been published to unanimously strong reviews. And of course for the previous six years Vidal had been a biting critic of George W. Bush and his wars in Iraq and Afghanistan—and in another year the Democrats would have a chance to replace him.*

Vidal arrived onstage, to prolonged applause from an enthusiastic audience, in a wheelchair pushed by a young man.

Vidal: Let me introduce the one pushing my wheelchair: my godson from France. They come in useful as they get older.

Q. Speaking of godchildren, you write in *Point to Point Navigation* that Tim Robbins and Susan Sarandon asked you to be the godfather of their new baby—and what was your answer?

A. Well, a little sob—and then: "always a godfather, never a god." [laughter]

Q. We are at a university, so I thought I would start by asking: why didn't you go to college? You may be the only person here in Royce Hall who didn't go to college.

A. I graduated from Exeter, and I was aimed at going to Harvard. Instead I enlisted in the army in 1943, and when I got out, in '46, I thought "I've spent all my life in institutions that I loathe, including my service in the Army of the United States." I thought, "Shall I go for another four years?" My first book was already being published, I was an old man of nineteen. I said "I'm going to be told how to write by somebody at Harvard." I said, "This is too great a risk."

But I did go there to lecture, this was about '47 or '48. There was a big audience, and many of them were my classmates from Exeter, who were over-age juniors and seniors in what looked to be their mid-forties. I came out cheerily, as is my wont, and I've never felt such hatred radiating. They'd all predicted my total failure, because I was not to go to Harvard and meet a publisher or an agent—which is, I think, why they went.

Q. You write in *Point to Point Navigation* that you were "once a famous novelist." I must disagree—you *are* a famous novelist. Look at this reception today.

A. "Famous novelist"—the adjective doesn't go with the noun. It's like being a famous speedboat designer: you can be a successful one, you can make a living out of it, but you're not famous. Fame is what the literary world was like before Mailer and I got into it. You had had people who were known all over the world, like Hemingway and Fitzgerald. I think we lost a lot of the audience for our team. Not "we" specifically. But the audience diminished in my lifetime.

Q. Your new memoir is titled *Point to Point Navigation*. Please explain the title.

A. I was first mate on an army boat up in the Aleutian Islands, and we had compasses, but we had no radar. This was '45, '46, and we couldn't set a course. We never saw the sun, or the moon, or stars. We just went point to point. And usually you would get an Aleut sailor,[1] get him to pledge to the ship, and he would know the whole coastline. We would go past this island and that island, to Chernovsky Point, where we were to dock.

I thought, "This is highly descriptive of my last forty years." Without a compass I'm just guessing, point by point. And as I remember points, I record them, for the future edification of others. It is one way of writing, one way of navigating. I wouldn't say it's the best, but you do what you can with what you've got. As the wise Secretary of Defense[2] said, "You fight the war with what you've got." Can you imagine something more insulting to everybody in the military? "They're no good, you know, but what can I do about it—I'm the head of a pharmaceutical company." I guess he's back with that now, selling aspirin over cost.

Q. You wrote a series of novels about American history. You called the series "Narratives of Empire." The books were *Burr, Lincoln, Washington DC, 1876, Empire*, which was on the 1890s, *Hollywood*, on the twenties, and *The Golden Age*, on America during and after World War II. It's hard to think of another writer who has written the entire history of his country this way.

A. I left out the Mexican War, and I'm going back to it: Henry Clay, President Polk, and our attack on Mexico, which didn't go down very well down there, as they return now to their stolen lands. [applause]

Q. The Mexican War was the one for which Thoreau went to jail in protest. Our anti-war protest tradition goes back that far.

A. Indeed it does. It is interesting today how few writers in their prime, as opposed to us octogenarians, spoke out against the terrible recent events in the Middle East—the Bush wars. James Wolcott is a clever writer for *Vanity Fair*. He wrote an interesting piece that said the only literary voices that have been raised against Iraq and Afghanistan are three veterans of World War II, all over 80: Mailer, Kurt Vonnegut and me.[3] And I thought, that was strange. We had already undergone a pretty awful war. I think we were more sensitive than somebody who had served underground in the Texas Air Force.[4]

Q. I wanted to stick with your fiction a little bit longer. The last of your Narratives of Empire series was titled *The Golden Age*. Do you really think the United States had a golden age?

A. It could have had, were it not for Harry Truman and the Korean War. I got out of the Army in '46, and suddenly all of the arts in the United States had taken off—arts that we never would have known about, like ballet. Suddenly there we were, with the ballet theater. It was a very exciting time, music was at its best, with people like Bernstein and Copeland. In the theater we had Tennessee Williams and Arthur Miller. And the novelists were not all that bad either.

My generation had been through the Depression, and then World War II. We were far from being the greatest generation, but we had certainly gone through the most tribulation. Then it was over, and I remember thinking as I got out of a bus near Times Square, "Well we don't have to do that again. We've had our war." Little knowing what time would yield.

All the arts were booming. It was just the most exciting time. New York was the center of the world—the center for painting, which it had never been before. There were things which had never been accessible to us which we suddenly became masters of, because there was all this energy left over from the war. I think a lot of us who had not gone to college had time to get going in the arts, which is what you should be doing at that age. So everything was glittering. Even TV, which was brand new and was loathed by many, but we thought something good might come out of it. And something did: live television drama, which was often "better than Broadway."

So here we were, right on the edge of a golden age, prepared to make a civilization, something the United States has never done. We were all dressed up with nowhere to go. Then in 1950, Harry Truman was looking forward to the Cold War, with a new enemy: Communism. He gets us into a disastrous war with Korea, which we promptly lose. And we have been at war ever since, and it has not done our character much good, and it hasn't been good for business either, except for Wall Street. That's what I say to the golden age. It was there, in ovum, but you have to sit on the egg, not step on it.

Q. You introduced the term "the America Empire" to journalism—not very popular at first, but now it seems indispensible.

A. *Time* magazine attacked me for a book of essays, saying, "He is the kind of essayist who refers to the American Empire." The whole magazine was shuddering with horror at what I'd said. A Brit came up with this one: "There is no American empire.

We had an empire in England, naturally, naturally we did, but you don't have one at all. What have you got? You've got Guam!" [laughter]

I said, "Yeah, but we've got Japan, and we've got Western Europe, and as much of Africa as we want, and as much of Latin America as we want." We had it all. And to see how this mess could be made in six years is beyond my ability to suspend belief. To have lost everything, and now the dollar too? At least we always had that to hang on to.

Q. 1968 was an exciting year in American politics and culture, and part of 1968 was *Myra Breckinridge*. In 1968 we got Nixon, and in 1968 we got Myra. It was a bestseller. I found a quote from Harold Bloom, *"Myra Breckinridge* seems to have fixed the limit beyond which the most advanced aesthetic neo-pornography never can go." My question is, how did you write that book? Where did Myra come from?

A. I don't know. I didn't invent cellophane, which I've always loved as an invention, but my father brought a big container of it home from Dupont. I was about eight or so, and I said, "What's it for?" He said, "Nobody knows, but isn't it beautiful?"

I think *Myra* is a bit the same. It came to me in Rome, when I was walking down an alley. Suddenly I hear this voice, booming in my ear: "Myra Breckinridge whom no man will ever possess." And I thought, "What is that?" This is the way a lot of comedy writing comes: you hear a voice, and you don't know what it means.

So I went on writing, and writing, and writing, and I was halfway through the book before I realized that Myra had been a man. Clever maker of fictional characters that I am, I thought no woman would sound like this.

Q. This year will be the 100th anniversary of the election of your grandfather, Thomas Pryor Gore, to the Senate. He was a populist, a supporter of William Jennings Bryan.[5] I learned from *Point to Point Navigation* that he was at war with Wall Street and the moneyed interests. Do you think there is a place for anyone like your grandfather in today's politics?

A. I'm auditioning.
[laughter]
   I think the Populist tradition has never died, and I think after Populism the next step was the New Deal, which is very much alive, I think, in people's psyche—the notion that you must do something for the people, or you don't really have a country. And, I do notice, we're losing more and more of the country. Don't you find it amazing? Where are the great voices? The Walter Lippmanns we had, at least in my youth, good journalists, wise men—where are their counterparts now when Habeas Corpus was released from the canon? Habeas Corpus, that's like the Magna Carta—one of the few good things England left us when they made their departure. And it's gone. Due process—where is that? The notion of the jury, which seems to get more and

more corrupted, as it's used as a government weapon to get rid of political parties that you do not enjoy. No, we are in danger of not having a country. We certainly aren't having a republic.

Senator T.P. Gore was elected in 1907 from the newly created state of Oklahoma. He had written a constitution for the state, and he was elected their first Senator. I come across a lot of people who think as he did. I went all through West Virginia not long ago, from Morgantown to Charles Town, speaking. It was like going back to my youth, because I was brought up in Virginia, in the eastern part, beyond Tidewater, so it was like a time warp— like being back in the thirties. Same people, same accents, same preoccupations. Perhaps our savior will come from Morgantown, West Virginia.

Q. So, your grandfather was in the Senate, and the grandfather of George W. Bush was in the Senate…

A. Very different. Very different people.

Q. Prescott Bush, Senator from Connecticut in the fifties.

A. Yes, he was Senator from J.P. Morgan. He was a creature of the House of Morgan. And Brown Brothers, which was a spin-off of the House of Morgan, was where a lot of Bush-ite mischief was done. May I tell you, Prescott Bush didn't figure at all in those days. He was unknown.

Q. So, we had Prescott Bush, the grandfather, who I guess now would now be called a liberal Republican; then we had George H. W. Bush, who would be more of a Nixon Republican; and now we have George W. Bush. Is there any historical trend here?

A. I don't think they are a dynasty we need bother with. I don't see much future for them. It's going to take four or five years to recover from this administration—to get the Constitution back, to get the legal codes back. They've done a lot of damage for a sort of nothing family.

Q. I wonder how you rank Bush 43 among the presidents. The *Washington Post* did a poll among historians asking who is the worst president, and it was sort of divided. Some said Bush 43, a lot said Nixon, one said Polk, for the Mexican War, one said Buchanan for not avoiding or anticipating the Civil War. What's your ranking of Bush among the worst presidents?

A. He wins. And now every day we see his victory dance on television.

Q. In the past decade you've been relatively critical of Al Gore, who is some sort of relative of yours, I'm not sure. I wonder what you think of the Al Gore of today, the Academy Award winner.[6]

A. This is an invention that I've been critical of him. Quite the contrary. I think that Arianna Huffington, on this very stage, said,

"Oh, you said such awful things about Al Gore." I said, "I don't say awful things about members of my family," and I was sorry about the way his election was hijacked in the year 2000. I think he should have fought a little harder, that was my only criticism. I now think that he is the only candidate now who has a real theme, which is the planet.

Q. Now that we've considered Al Gore's candidacy for the Presidency, of course I have to ask you about what you think of the other leaders of our opposition party: Hillary, Obama, John Edwards.

A. Oh splendid, all splendid. Look, anything to get rid of this Bush gang.
[applause]

Q. Anything else you'd like to say about Hillary?

A. I like her. She said something interesting when she was getting ready to run for Senator in New York—my own private advice was to go to Illinois and become Governor. Chicago is a much better city, I think, to launch yourself from. Anyway, she was going through where she was popular. She was most unpopular among white men with some property. She was asking, "What have I done to them?" And she kept on with some of her advisors, I am told—I didn't get this firsthand. And she was told, "It is because you remind them of their first wife."
[laughter]

Q. Let's talk about Iraq for a second. With all the emphasis on the stupidity of Bush's war, and of the Coalition Provisional Authority, headed by Paul Bremer, the implication is that if we had more troops there, if we had people running this war who understood the Middle East, if we hadn't had these Republican ideologues running the reconstruction, we could have succeeded in building "a democratic Iraq." I wonder what you think about that.

A. First you would have had to have had a democratic war, in which the people have something to say. We didn't have anything to say.

We had no business fighting in Iraq. It was only though a series of lies that the war got as far as it did in Congress. It was all nonsense. What we do is relentlessly search for enemies; we've been doing it now for many, many years, but it's never been so highly developed as with this gang.

The point is that we should not have gone to war. This is no business of ours. I love the last minute idea of, "Oh, we are going to bring democracy to Iraq!" "It's a fledgling democracy," says the little fellow. What a fledgling! It looks more like a goose to me—one gently cooking and simmering.

I'm beginning to have a theory. I wrote a play in 1962, based on one by Friedrich Dürrenmatt, about Romulus the Great, the last Roman emperor. He had become an Emperor in order to destroy the Roman Empire, because it had been immoral and bloodthirsty. He had become Emperor for one purpose—to destroy Rome and its armies. I think we've got another one. I think the little fellow, instinctively, knew he was never going to measure up to a real president like Roosevelt, or even to his father. So he has wrecked everything that he touches.

To wreck the United Nations, he gets Mr. Bolton[7] to go there, who hates it and wants to destroy it. Look at what he does with the army: he gets a pharmaceutical freak to play warlord of the Pentagon, and that just doesn't work. "Heck of a job, Brownie."[8] He gets people who don't know how to save a city from a flood. Whatever he does is a mess. Now that takes mind—and probably a plan.

Q. Let's go to questions from the audience.

From the audience:

Q. I'd like you to comment on the healthcare in this country, because you are sitting in a wheelchair, and I am without my front teeth.

A. Madam, I see no connection.
[laughter]

From the audience:

Q. I've been a fan of yours since the 60's, when you used to do those great debates with William F. Buckley[9]. I was wondering if you would consider doing those kinds of debates again. I'd pay good money to see them.

A. I'd pay good money not to do them.
[laughter]

Questioner 2, cont. Also, I was wondering if you had a comment on the recent passing of Buckley's wife, Pat Buckley, who died a few days ago.

A. I liked her. She was very nice. Long suffering. When I was speaking in West Virginia in Charles Town, the capital of the state, to an audience about like this, someone asked a question from the audience: "When Buckley called you what he did on television, why didn't you belt him one?" I said, "I've done many wrong things in my life—but I have never decked a lady."
[laughter]

Q. I'd like to ask the last question. In your career you've done it all: novels, essays, film, television. You've won all the big awards. What keeps you going? What gets you up in the morning?

A. Rage.

Q. Thank you, Gore Vidal!

Los Angeles Institute for the Humanities
University of Southern California
Dec. 15, 2006

The Los Angeles Institute for the Humanities is a group of 100 or so that brings together academics with independent writers, artists and critics. Modeled on the better-known New York Institute of the Humanities, it meets monthly during the academic year at USC, although faculty members come also from UCLA and other area campuses. The meetings include lunch followed by a talk, followed by questions and comments. Usually the talks are by fellows describing their new projects, but sometimes outsiders are invited—Joan Didion, Pico Iyer, Alex Ross, Michael Kinsley.

Vidal's audience included theater director Gordon Davidson, Getty Museum Director John Walsh, Getty Research Institute director Thomas Crow, Time film critic Richard Schickel, novelist Marianne Wiggins (wife of Salmon Rushdie), and UCLA historians Joyce Appleby and Eugen Weber.

Vidal arrived wearing a Harvard athletic letter jacket.

Vidal: I didn't go to Harvard, but I have gone on, as you can see, to be a professor of Harvard. I was in a terrible movie in which

I played a Harvard professor.[1] This is the winter wear there. I am now on a secret visit to the Southland, examining the facilities of the community colleges, and that is why I am here at USC today. [laughter]

Q. As a matter of fact, there is a fascinating passage in *Point to Point Navigation*, where you write that Paul Bowles,[2] who was preparing to teach at Cal State Northridge—this must have been sometime in the late 1940's—asked you the night before his first class how you teach writing. What was all this about?

A. I don't think his students ever found out. Paul himself was very vague. He said, "What is a class?" He had this extraordinary literal mind that he learned from Gertrude Stein, who was his first mentor when he was just out of, or on the lam from, the University of Virginia. She told him, "You're not a poet, you better be a musician, it's easier." So he went to study with Virgil Thomson and Aaron Copeland, and became a very distinguished musician, and then went back to writing, and wrote rather better than Ms. Stein. But that was all in the future. But no, our subject was community colleges. I am delighted: they are springing up all over.

Q. One of the things they do at community colleges is teach fiction writing. I think there are programs everywhere now. At my school, U.C. Irvine, we have an undergraduate major called "Literary Journalism." It started only a couple of years ago, but it already has over 200 majors, and if there are 200 at Irvine, there is a similar number at a hundred other schools. This means hundreds of thousands of students are studying to be writers. What do you make of this?

A. We have Truman Capote to thank for that. As bad writers go, he took the cake. So bad was he, you know, he created a whole new art form: the nonfiction novel. He had never heard of a tautology, he had never heard of a contradiction. His social life was busy.

To have classes in fiction—that really is hopeful, isn't it. People can go to school and bring in physics. The genius of Thomas Pynchon's *Gravity's Rainbow*: He had to take all of his first year courses at, what was it, Cornell? One of his teachers was Nabokov. And everything he had in his first year's physics went in to *Gravity's Rainbow*. Whether it fit in or not, it just went in there. That's one way of doing it.

Q. In *Point to Point Navigation*, you start by saying you were "once a famous novelist." Were there famous novelists in the forties and fifties?

A. More so than now, yeah. When I gave the Massey Lectures at Harvard,[3] I had mostly graduate students in the audience, very bright. A great many Chinese from mainland China, who know a great bit more about American civilization than the locals know. So it was quite a treat talking to them. But I noticed something interesting whenever I took on a class at Harvard, undergraduate,

29

post graduate, whatever: no one ever mentioned a book, or a poem, or anything to do with literature. They're interested in our history, they're interested in our politics. But I finally broke the ice with my Chinese friends. I said, has anybody here seen *The Doors*?[24] Well the whole room fell apart. Everybody had seen *The Doors*. I got away with a hour without having to do anything while they told me about *The Doors*. That's fame, alas.

Q. You wrote a series of novels about American history. You call the series "Narratives of Empire." They start with the revolutionary era and *Burr* and conclude seven novels later with *The Golden Age*, which is about the forties and fifties. It is hard to think about another writer who has written the entire history of his country in this way.

A. And it's also hard to think of a reader in the United States, including those who pass as critics, who would read it. This is just off the map. Literature is supposed to be about merit, and there is nothing else that matters on earth. If you have values. Now, it's always about somebody trying to get tenure in Ann Arbor, and his wife leaves him because of that au pair from England, and the child is autistic, and we have a lot of hospital scenes that are heartbreaking. And this goes on, and on, and on. I once had to judge the National Book Awards. There was no fiction in it—there was nothing. There was certainly no literature in it. It was just "write about what you know." And what they knew wasn't very much. At least with me you'll find out who was Buchanan's Vice President.

[laughter]

Okay, I'm tooting my own horn.

Q. On the subject of writing about what you know, you introduced the term "The American Empire", I think, into polite society, and polite society wasn't too happy about it initially.

A. I was born in the lair of Romulus and Remus, Washington D.C. I was right there at the beginning, at the heart of it. My grandfather was blind from the age of ten, and I lived with him until I was 17 when I went into the army. I would take him down to the Senate and act as his page, and it was the engine room of the Republic. We were a Republic turning military. The Second World War was beginning, and the town was flooded with Brits. There was something like 11,000 of them, I've been told. Some of the brightest people in England, starting with Isaiah Berlin, they were all there, to try and get us in the war to save England from Hitler. France had just fallen, I'm speaking now of the spring of 1940. And I understood perfectly well what an empire was. I had also been reading a lot of Roman history. I was fascinated. The first grown-up book I read was *Stories From Livy*, a 19th-century edition, which got me into the Republic, and then later the Empire surrounded us all.

It was a great time to be an observant kid in the position of a fly on the wall. My mother was a leading isolationist/hostess in the town—Mrs. Auchincloss, she was called[5]—and Senator Gore was anti-Roosevelt, anti-going-to-war. He had opposed World War I, and was one of 80 per cent of people that did not want to go to war in Europe again. These were fierce years, this was a fierce debate.

I was head of the America First group at Exeter.[6] Arthur Schlesinger Jr. always thought he could rile me by saying, "Oh, you know about Gore, he's an isolationist." Of course I was, you idiot! And so was every right-thinking young man on the left. Everybody from Norman Thomas to Senator Burton Wheeler,[7] all the progressives in the United States were anti-war. This is something left out by many historians. We have always been a nation devoted to the principles of George Washington. Nations do not have particular friends or enemies, only interests— a nice mercantile piece of advice that most intellectuals accepted; Charles Beard as well, master of your discipline, was also on that side. It was highly respectable. Then "isolationist" became a word for anyone who—well, who had been abducted by aliens in the backyard, had seen a world elsewhere and didn't like it much.

Q. As an America Firster in 1940, you weren't on the left. How did you go from being an Exeter America Firster to being a critic of the empire?

A. Just lucky.
[laughter]

No, I knew it was a bad notion. I took Washington's farewell address seriously. I took seriously John Quincy Adams' Fourth of July address of 1824: America is not a nation that goes forth to foreign lands to kill dragons. We fight under no banner other than that of our own, even though it be compatible with liberty, freedom, justice, and all that. Yes we could do this, we could become dictator of the world. And we would lose our own soul. I was much moved by that, and stuck with it.

Q. Your grandfather, Senator Gore, was from Oklahoma, a Populist state. Did you visit Oklahoma? You were a Washington D.C. boy.

A. I didn't like the empire, but I liked being in Rome. [laughter] I never set foot in Oklahoma until I was grown. I had to go to the army, then I went south of the border, and went on writing in Guatemala, in time to be there during the preparations by Ambassador Peurifoy[8] to overthrow the government of Arbenz, democratically elected, because he wanted to put a small tax on United Fruit. And Mario Monteforte Toledo, President of their Assembly, and Vice President of the country, had an Indian girlfriend in Antigua, and he would come up on weekends, and we would always argue politics. He would talk about "yanqui imperialismo," and I would always say, "The United States is not like that." I didn't know what he was talking about. He would say, "No, your government is prepared to overthrow us. I shall end up in exile." I said, "Well, look, we've just conquered—we've just appropriated Japan and Germany. What do we want Guatemala for?" But he just knew instinctively that we were piggish, and needed a little fruit for our diet. That was to be the big banana for us.[9]

And so it came to pass. Arévalo was replaced democratically by a great believer in our constitution, and in Franklin Roosevelt—Jacobo Arbenz, who became President. And that's when we called in the C.I.A to overthrow the government, and replace him with a fellow called Armas, who began a bloodbath that continues till this day.[10] If that is not an empire, I don't know what is.

Q. On the one hand, we have your books about American history, but you've also written a very different kind of book, of which *Myra Breckinridge* is my favorite. 1968 gave us Nixon, and 1968 gave us Myra. We know where Nixon came from, but where did Myra come from?

A. William F. Buckley, Jr. [laughter] I needed some model. And, some of you may remember, I debated him on television. At the '68 Convention in Chicago, and also in Miami at the Republican Convention, and he was just out of his mind with fury at whatever was going on. And I realized that here was a true American. I called him a "crypto-Nazi" because I couldn't think of the word "fascist." We were talking very quickly. Anyway, I take it all back now. He's a very pure nothing. [laughter] I was doing him the honor of superimposing a system on him, a mind where none was present.

Q. Myra loved film, yet the film of *Myra Breckinridge* was, let us say, not a success. What went wrong there?

A. It was produced by the wrong people. I think that is usually what goes wrong. They are drawn to unusual novels, sometimes even classics. They'll go after *The Great Gatsby*, which is a lovely novel. They'll go, many times, after *Anna Karenina*. Nobody going after it understands why it's marvelous: it's marvelous because there is a personal voice, which is the author's. They don't allow that there is an author. Grudgingly they say that the director is an auteur, but they wink at you when they say that because they know perfectly well that it is the producer's brother-in-law who did the last script. And got credit.

Forgive me for this, but Hollywood film is a medium basically without a mind. It's not a functioning mind, and it's not a communicative mind. Minds can create it, but it's essentially moving pictures, which are made to move you, and which are emotional. It's very good at terror, pity, awe; but it can't make you think.

You know, the French are a people who love cinema far, far too much. Their favorite is—and this I suppose is also mine—*Battleship Potemkin*. There is a scene in it that is just magical for them, I mean they look like they've just seen Bernadette at Lourdes when you mention it.[11] And it's the baby in the buggy going bumpety-bump-bump-bump down the steps, after the *Potemkin* has rebelled against the government. Next time they pull that on you, you pull this one on them: Tell me what that scene means. What does it have to do with the Revolution?

The movie's supposedly about that. It doesn't mean anything. And movies can do that all too easily. We prose writers with flat pages have great difficulty in trying to recreate bumpety-bump-bumps.

Q. If we're talking about movies, I have to ask about Fellini's. You have a wonderful chapter about Fellini in the book. You appear in Fellini's *Roma*, one of his greatest films. Do you think Fellini was subject to the same limitations?

A. He wasn't without limits, but he was essentially a painter. He did not like direct sound, so he never used it, as far as I know. He hated scripts, as far as I know he never really used one. The studio gave him one, and he would take it and pretend to make it. Direct sound and in English is how he got his money, and that's the thing he never did. I used to argue with him about it all the time. He would tell me, "It's very difficult to get money now." I would say, "Well, your pictures don't make any money." He would say, "It's not possible, look at the awards I got," this award and that award. I said, "They like to give you awards, but they're not going to give you money because they'll lose it. They're strange people, aren't they."

He was a wildly funny guy. At his best he was one of the greatest liars of all time. I noticed a Mr. Schickel in the room, who may have interviewed him.[12] And others here may have interviewed him. The one word he hated, if you wanted him to go up the wall on you, would be "why." There is no answer to "why?" And if there was, he was not going to tell you.

Q. We've lasted a half hour without mentioning George Bush, which I think is quite an achievement. But we need to mention George Bush. The *Washington Post* had a symposium where they rounded up a bunch of historians and asked them who was the worst President. It usually comes down to a contest between Nixon and Bush, although there was one essay that was titled "He's Only the Fifth Worst"—you know the argument: Nixon did some good things and Bush did nothing good.[13] I'm wondering if you would be interested in joining the "who is the worst President" debate.

A. I'd probably start, if you really want to be serious, with Woodrow Wilson. Imagine taking us to a war in Europe for nothing. We had no interests there, got no advantages out of it, and tens of thousands of Americans were killed. We got Prohibition out of it, and that was about it. And guess what his slogan was: "to make the world safe for democracy." It's like making the world safe for good temper. It's as idiotic as that.

He had spent two seasons in the Lake District of England and had become an Anglophile. If he'd just gone back there to once again read Wordsworth and left the troops at home. Instead he redesigns Europe. He never took geography in kindergarten, he didn't know where anything was. He broke up the only stable thing in Central Europe, the Austria-Hungarian empire. In order to create Yugoslavia?

Sigmund Freud was in such a rage. We like to think of him as a great genius of serene and august temperament. But Freud was so furious he did the most unprofessional thing ever done by any psychiatrist, much less a founder. He wrote a psychoanalysis of Woodrow Wilson without ever having met him. And he got all the details, mostly slanderous, from Bill Bullitt, a fifth-rate ambassador that President Roosevelt was sending around Europe. Oh, you should read it, it's just fantasy gone mad. The great doctor was crazy with anger, he saw that the only stability in Europe, particularly the Europe of the Jews, was the Austro-Hungarian empire and its capital, Vienna. From there to Prague, that was a safety zone for Jews. At the end it was in shambles. So I think we must give Wilson a private place for number one.

Q. The big puzzle to me about George W. Bush is that his father represents a more traditional kind of American ruling entity, which indeed was wiser about what could be accomplished, and what couldn't, in a place like Iraq. George Bush 41 comes from the milieu of your family, and had a more reasonable view of the world than his son, it seems.

A. I would not want to have to be immodest and check the IQ of any Bush against that of any Gore. [laughter] I do not mean to boast, but I think we're well ahead in that desperate race. No, George Bush Sr. was just about as dumb as the son, but he took the education of a gentleman seriously, and as much as he could, behaved like one. Remember, he enlisted in the army, he was a pilot, a hero in the war—except for the two flight members who had to bail out. We never heard their story. I believe Kitty Kelley is working on it now.[14] Soon we'll know his last words to them were "bye-bye." [laughter] That's what they said about him at Andover, you know, when it was all over.

Q. I know we have many people here who would like to ask questions.

From the audience:

Q. You've written many books, and they've been reviewed many times, including in the *New York Times*. What reviews that you have received seem to you now to be the most interesting, or even the most helpful in causing you to rethink your work?

A. I'm more apt to rethink the *New York Times* than I am to rethink my work. I'd say the piece I most liked, and admittedly it was admiring, was Harold Bloom on *Lincoln* and on my approach to American history. There is a wonderful German word that I've tried to make popular, when I can remember it: "Einfuehlen." That is the ability to work your way into the past, never forgetting you're in a foreign country. It isn't the present with new decorations, it's another place. It's another world. If you can keep that sense of strangeness as you work, then you've got half the job done. But I find most American writers lack Einfuehlen. They're not very good at being naturalistic writers either, which means that they have a hard time with their own surroundings. Due to the, you know, rigors of getting tenure at Ann Arbor, which I've already referred to. As for the negative stuff about me: consider the source.

Audience Q. Your observation about the changes in the meaning of the word narcissism: I wonder if you'd talk about that.

A. As it's used now, narcissist means a fag. I tried to give it a deeper meaning. I was helping out some book reviewer. I said "a narcissist is anyone better looking than you are." [laughter] I think that struck a nerve, because I've had people come up to me on the street, keening, howling, over that. Still suffering over that blow.

Follow-up Q. You go on to make the point about how the word is now sometimes associated with liberals.

A. Yes, narcissistic liberals. Because they want to help others, and not themselves. The height of narcissism. But then altruism has never had a big market for the freedom clan. I thought you were going to quote me on altruism. I thought that wasn't too bad. I said, "Altruism is a bit like acne, it hits many people in different ways. It hits the young, often in adolescence, but luckily usually leaves no scars."

Audience Q. I read a recent piece about your book, in which you were quoted as saying the only times you've been completely happy have been at the movies. Watching movies. I am wondering if you could explain the origins of that happiness.

A. Oh, it was generational. I was born at the time when the talkies first came in, and I was fourteen years old in the greatest year of the talking picture, 1939. I saw them all, and it was bliss to have been fourteen then, seeing the *Wizard of Oz*. That was all I meant by that. I did not mean I get that feeling going to see Monsieur Mel Gibson, the famous French auteur. No, I don't feel it in later cases.

Audience Q. I was curious about how easily the American electorate is manipulated in all kinds of ways. As somebody who is a member of a democracy of some sort, some crude sort, how do you deal with that? Jefferson thought we really shouldn't be an electoral democracy, you know, a one man-one vote kind of thing. How do you look upon the future of this country with any optimism, when how blatantly manipulated a great deal of the electorate is—like people who vote against their economic interests in Ohio, etc, etc.

A. Well the only optimists are the gas and oil people, and they have every reason to be. It has always been the trick of our republic to get people to vote wholeheartedly against their interests. That's very exciting when you can do it. [laughter] I remember when I was running for Congress upstate New York, in Duchess Country, and there would be these farmers going around in old, old, Model-T Fords and so on, with stickers—Vote for Rockefeller. Sometimes I would stop them, and we'd chat. I'd say, "Why do you like him?" because he was pretty poisonous even then. They said, "He's so rich he wouldn't steal our money."

I said, "That wouldn't stop him. Rich people go right on robbing people you know." He was spending a lot of money up in Albany. He has his grand pyramid, he has his sphinx, all types of things up there to remind people of the Rockefellers.[15] And I couldn't get a straight answer out of them.

I asked, "Do you think you'll get a check out of him someday? Or, like his grandfather, he'll give you a dime?" A lot of people out there could be bought for a dime. I remember when I was running for the House, Republicans since time immemorial had bought votes in the district. And the price had gone up in 1960 to about $15, which is a hell of a lot of money up there. And particularly in nearby Tivoli, which I lived not too far from.

My campaign manager was Judge Hawkins, a wonderful guy. He was head of the Democratic Party up there. He said, "They're going to beat us because of the bought votes."

And I, a perfect Populist, said, "Why don't we buy them too? Just pay a few dollars more?" I understand the workings of the market. That's how it works. That's why I proposed myself for office in the great republic, for deals in business. He said, "They always catch us, they never catch them." And that man was a judge.

Audience Q. I read *Myra Breckinridge* a long time ago, I remember it absolutely wowed me because it seemed so sexually perverse, but absolutely brilliant. It's been forty years since you wrote *Myra*, yet America seems to have become more puritanical. Do you have any sort of insights on where America might be heading on accepting more sexual pluralism?

A. I think what you have now is a combination of advertising, which is essentially erotic. And we had a drug generation for a time, which perhaps encouraged sexual activity. I don't know what the changes have been, but forget all about values. I don't see the freedoms that we enjoyed back in the '60's, they have not been translated into political action, nor have they had much of any effect, that I can tell.

But we are a funny country: we've always had more good writers than good readers. So here we are, a bunch of writers just sort of marooned in limbo with nobody to read the things. Just passing asteroids. With other countries, if you have writers, you have readers. We have writers, we can't get anyone to read them. The theory of American publishing today is "print and pulp, print and pulp, print and pulp," as quickly as possible, to have room for another to "print and pulp."

The intermediary time, which might have been used for marketing—I know I sound like a merchant, but we've got to sell something—should have been used to get people to read. Also look at what the schools do. Those who even take up literature at all, they removed Shakespeare—it's too difficult for the curriculum. It used to be you had to read *Julius Caesar* at least, because there was no sex in it. It's not my reading of what happened with Cassius and Brutus, which could have been a very hot scene, but anyway—in the eye of the beholder is the beholden.

Audience Q. Is God a Republican? I mean, if you were writing that book, would it be in the sci-fi section? The comic section?

Who could write about what is going on now? And would anyone believe it?

A. I think I could have thought it up. It's not difficult, you know. I mean, it's so easy to propagandize. 70 per cent believed, and still believe, that Saddam Hussein was working hand in glove with Osama bin Laden. They hated each other, and that is known everywhere but in the land of the free, where nothing is known. And nothing is known because the media is so poisonous and so controlled.

And they say, "The people are dumb." No, they're not dumb, they are ignorant. They have no access to information. Or they get so much access they don't know what to believe and end up believing nothing. I think, as a writer fifteen years ago, I would have been more interested in that subject—how you turn people off the whole idea of learning anything at all through reading.

I remember when *Burr* first published. I had a great friend in the business, very bright woman. I introduced her to Edith Wharton and she never looked back, so she is a good reader when she wants to be. She said, "Oh, I got your book," and I said, "But you're not going to read it." She said, "How did you know?"

I said, "Why not?" And she said, "Well, I don't know who Aaron Burr is." I replied, "That's the idea! If you already knew, why would I have written a book?" This was beyond her.

Everyone here has written journalism. You're up against it all the time: no one knows who that person is—so why write a book about them? Why write a piece about them? Nobody knows them. But that's the reason for writing, isn't it. Difficult thought, difficult thought. Only write about what you already know. So we've got Elizabeth Taylor until the end of time.

Audience Q. If you could look back over the course of a life, what do you think have been the major factors that contributed to the rise in political apathy?

A. Apathy is just lack of energy, which to me, is just the literal definition of decadence. So the energy gives out in a society—that is decadence. We gave out some time ago. If it were just in the culture—literature and so on, music—ok, ok, we can play other games. But it's gone out of everything. It was outsourced. And apathy came in from India, and we've got apathy in every street corner. Our old get-up-and-go-ness has gone to Bangladesh.

Follow-up Q. But why?

A. Society's changed. Capitalism, if we want to get down to it, as Marx put it. You can make widgets cheaper in poor countries, so we go to poor countries to make them, depriving our own people of livelihood. If we had labor unions we might be able to change that, but we've done away with them because they stood in the way of Republican majorities. So, there is work to be done politically.

Q. Our time is almost up, I'm going to ask the last question. At this point in your life you've done it all. You've written almost two dozen books, you've won all the prizes, you've done the movies, the plays. What keeps you going?

A. All my life I've been over-excited by stupidity. Just before I came here I was listening to the leader of the free world eulogizing the great man of the Iraq war as the greatest Secretary of Defense in history. We used to call him the Secretary of War, before the dumb-dumbs took over, and then after 1948 it became Defense, once we decided we were going to be at war all the time. Too much overlap. All I have to do is turn on CNN now, and I have to say, I'm rolling on the floor.

3 The 2000 Shadow Convention: Radio Interview
Plaza Hotel, New York City
September 9, 2000

Vidal was in New York City in September, 2000, for the revival of his play The Best Man, *which that year starred Charles Durning, Spalding Gray, and Chris Noth. The interview ostensibly was for KPFK radio in Los Angeles, where I had a show, but we talked much too long for that, an hour and twenty minutes, and the station ended up broadcasting only excerpts. He invited me to do the interview in his suite at the Plaza Hotel, where he and his partner Howard Austen were staying. When I arrived, he was wearing the hotel white terrycloth robe, and I had some difficulty finding a place attach the microphone for our new Digital Audio Recorder.*

It was a big season for Gore: not only was his play being revived on Broadway, but the final novel of his "Empire" series, The Golden Age, *had just been published. And of course we were in the middle of the Bush v. Gore political campaign, and many on the left were supporting Ralph Nader, arguing that there was little difference between Gore and Bush.*

Q. The last time I saw you in Los Angeles, a month ago [August 2000], you were standing on the back of a flatbed truck downtown on Figueroa Avenue, as the Democratic Convention was reaching its climax three blocks away. You had been scheduled as a speaker at the Shadow Convention, a left-wing alternative to the DNC, but the police had ordered an evacuation of the building where you were to speak. Hundreds of people had gathered in the street around this flatbed truck; the LAPD's finest had lined up, in riot gear, batons at the ready, at both ends of the block; and you were addressing the assembled crowd. What was that like for you?

A. After all, I lived through the wars in Chicago in 1968, when the police rioted, and I saw disturbing similarities between 1968 and 2000. However, the Los Angeles Police Department was pretty clever. As you know, they have their own foreign policy, and their own C.I.A., and no doubt a unit to remove from the sphere with extreme prejudice certain individuals. Obviously they had decided that Ms. Huffington's Shadow Convention should not take place.

The Shadow Convention was for speakers whose views did not go along with the establishment of the county and were going to say things opposite to what was being said at the Democratic Convention. We were going to talk about, among other things, legalizing drugs. A lot of them were for Nader, and it might have been quite interesting. I arrived there, Christopher Hitchens was there. We sat and we talked, and we waited and we waited. I wondered why we were waiting. There were 600 people in the hall, people who had come to take part in the Shadow Convention. We waited and waited, and nobody seemed to know what was happening, except that we knew nothing was happening.

Then Ms. Huffington came in to tell us that there had been a bomb report—that a bomb had been set in the building and we could not go on. So we sat and discussed that. And this seemed a very unlikely thing, but you never know. We live in a very dangerous world. Then the word came that we were to evacuate the building—this was presumably great-heartedness on the part of the police, to save these vile people who did not celebrate the American way of life as does the LAPD.

So we left the building, and there was no place to go but the sidewalk, where there was a truck with sound equipment on the back—microphones and so on—so we go down there, and everybody gathers on the sidewalk, but some of them move out into Figueroa. And I was asked to amuse the crowd as the police, as you have so beautifully and chillingly described, marched by us, two by two, with plastic visors over their faces, carefully designed so you couldn't see who they were. And they went marching into the building, with a kind of S.S. stride.

So there I am, trying to amuse the audience—we can't really get into anything substantive. I spoke and I handed the microphone to Christopher Hitchens who said—I wish I had said it: "Do you really think that if there was a bomb in there, the police would have gone in and run the risk of getting hurt? If indeed there was a bomb in there, specialists would have been sent in long ago, because if this place were blown up, it is close enough to also blow up the convention center," where all the Democrats were gathered.

We all thought this was terribly good deductive reasoning, very Hitchenseque.

Then two by two the police marched out of the building and said we could go back in. By this time shades of evening had fallen upon the group, and I went home.

The day before I had gone to the town hall meeting that *The Nation* magazine had held in a synagogue in Brentwood, which had been a rather exciting affair with Senator Wellstone, and Jesse Jackson's son, a congressman, and the usual suspects were there. It was a good meeting.

Q. The next morning Arianna Huffington said at a press conference that 100 members of the LAPD had shown up to protect the citizens of Los Angeles from Gore Vidal.

A. She said that?

Q. Yes.

A. I am flattered, naturally. But I wouldn't be a bit surprised. I was co-chair of the People's Party[1] and I have a house in the Hollywood Hills. We were carefully monitored—who came to the house and so on. I was told never to drive myself, always to be driven, because they would try to arrest you on traffic offenses, something or other they'll trump up. Also back in '68 they would do things like reach into the car and pick up a marijuana blunt. They would have had it in their own hand and then reach in and say, ah, look what we found. I have been driven around Los Angeles ever since. If they recognize you and you are against the policies of the LAPD nation, you better watch out.

Q. This is a big season for Gore Vidal: your twenty-fourth novel, *The Golden Age*, is being published. A revival of your play, *The Best Man*, is opening on Broadway. I saw a preview last night and was on the edge of my seat thinking, how is this going to end? There aren't very many plays that give you that feeling nowadays.

A. I wrote it in 1959, and it opened forty years ago at the Morosco Theater. And in those days one thought a play, particularly one that had political ideas and machinations, ought to be interesting. I think we were more devoted to interesting an audience, which is best done by revelations of character that surprise an audience. It must be a fair surprise, because you must prepare for it, which takes the kind of energy that the average playwright doesn't seem to want to expend or even care for.

Somebody wrote that *The Best Man* was the last of the well-made plays. It was a phrase of compliment for many years, and then it became one of derision. A well-made play of course was one that had no content, a sort of mechanical thing put together by a carpenter. After all, we are called playwrights; we aren't called poets. The theater changed in the early sixties. We got marvelous figures, generally from abroad, like Beckett and Ionesco. And the realistic play just withered. It either became the heart of commercialism, or it just went away entirely. I don't think it was cause and effect, but Broadway folded. In the season of 1960-1961 there were about forty plays on Broadway, and I don't think there's hardly one anymore.

Q. *The Golden Age* is about America in the forties and fifties. In some ways, the title is ironic because this is the age of Pearl Harbor, Hiroshima, Joe McCarthy, but also, briefly toward the end, you portray a sort of cultural renaissance, at least in New York in the forties and fifties, of which *The Best Man* was a part, not to mention your novels.

A. When we won the Second World War, or rather when the Russians beat the Germans on the ground, and we beat the Japanese by air and by sea, we and the Russians were allies, and we could have gone on being allies, were it not for a series of sinister events. Between 1945 and 1950 there were five years, the only five years since Pearl Harbor, the only five years out of sixty, until very recently, that we were not at war. Cold wars, tepid wars, hot wars. We've been through about seventy or eighty wars since Pearl Harbor. None of them declared by Congress, naturally, because not even Congress today would have signed off on them.

Our golden age for the arts in New York was just spectacular. We suddenly shot to the top of the world in ballet, something we had never done before—before that we had been just imitations of European ballet. Suddenly there was Jerome Robbins, there was Agnes de Mille. Then there was the age of the great musical. *Oklahoma, Kiss Me Kate*—every week there was a new musical coming along, most of them classics by now. In the theater, one week you'd have a new Tennessee Williams, *A Streetcar Named Desire*, then Arthur Miller's *Death of a Salesman* the next week. The plays of Bill Inge.[2] The theater was never so alive. And we just thought that this was normal, we knew that things had been flat during the war, because people were away (including the audience) and when we got home, there was all this pent-up energy.

And then the novel: in 1948, number one on the bestseller list was George Orwell's *1984*. Number two was Norman Mailer, *The Naked and the Dead*. Capote and I were around four and five on the list, and a half dozen other marvelous novelists of the period were on the bestseller list. I'm not just talking about being published, but they were being read. And, of course, it proved to be the beginnings of the golden age of poetry. Robert Lowell, Randall Jarrell, Elizabeth Bishop.

In writing *The Golden Age*, I try to remember what we ate, where did we go to eat, and who said what to whom—and what Dawn Powell[3] was like when she was well and truly drunk, and well and truly brilliant. I have a very nice aria of Dawn Powell giving her real opinion of her friend Hemingway, it is absolutely devastating. Part of it is direct quotes I found in letters of Dawn Powell giving her view about how unlucky Hemingway was to have survived his plane crash in Africa, because he got to read

53

all of his obituaries. And of course, you know "a great oak has fallen leaving a hole in the sky where it once bloomed and blossomed…" She said now poor Ernest, having read these marvelous obituaries, is going to have bad press until the end of his life, and will never be allowed to read the bad obituaries he is going to get later on, everyone had sort of shot their wad with Hemingway.

But it was a great time. American literature, for once, was now being recognized around the world. Europeans had been cut off from us by war and fascism, and the communist system did not allow much literature in. It wasn't so good for people like Mailer and me—we were too new. They were just catching up on Hemingway and Fitzgerald. John Dos Passos, the Europeans really liked that season. American literature was all over Europe, and it had never been before. People like Camus and Sartre were translating American writers, and we were translating them.

So, for five years we had the beginning of a golden age, and my book's title is essentially ironic, because five years does not make an age, but it suggests what an age might have been, had it been left alone.

But Harry Truman happened to us. Roosevelt died in 1945. Truman became President. Dean Acheson—I think evil is a good word for him—became, at least in action, his Prime Minister, or Secretary of State. And they talked themselves into two things. One, believing that the Russians were coming—that they were our enemies, that Stalin was a vicious dictator, all of which was true—except the Russians were not coming.

The Russians wanted to live by Yalta, the last meeting that Roosevelt had with Stalin and Churchill.[4] And then a few things happened. Roosevelt died, and Truman became President. He didn't know anything about foreign affairs, he didn't even know about the atom bomb. They had a second meeting with the Russians planned, at Potsdam. Truman goes there, ready to just give it to the Russians, because they weren't living up to their agreements in Poland and so on. But they were trying to live up to them, and we had agreed at Yalta that Germany would be governed by the four powers—France, Britain, Soviet Union, the U.S.—jointly. And the Russians never backed off from the Yalta agreement. We did. And we did because while the meeting was going on, Truman got a message from Los Alamos that the atom bomb worked, which meant we didn't need Russia. There was still a war going on with Japan, but we didn't need Russia. He used that as an excuse to break the agreement, Roosevelt's agreement, with Stalin. And we became obstinate, we wouldn't agree to anything.

In no time at all we divide Germany, and Stalin, horrified, immediately denied us access to Berlin, and then came the Berlin airlift, which we got through without too much damage done us, but the damage done our relationship with the Soviet Union was total, as was intended.

Truman, with Acheson, had decided to have what Charles Beard called "perpetual war for perpetual peace."[5] When he militarized the economy we had a permanent enemy: communism. By 1950 we were back on a wartime footing, and North Korea invaded South Korea, Truman didn't even dare ask Congress for a declaration of war that soon after Hitler had been defeated, so he called it a UN police action. The draft was back in peacetime. Imagine, a draft. The income tax was high. They took all the money, they put it in armaments. We started NATO, we started the C.I.A. We started a lot of secret police.

So that was 1950, that was the end of the golden age. Then McCarthy comes, and the blacklist, and people are living in a police state. And with no redress, because the national security state is not representative, it is an imposed state of affairs. It is military, and it is hierarchical. The people were then excluded. And that is the world, my friends, that we have been living in for the last fifty years.

Q. The Golden Age starts in 1940, and very much like your play *The Best Man*, which is set in 1960, a political convention is front and center at the beginning of the novel. Both conventions, the 1940 Republican Convention, which we visit in *The Golden Age*, and a hypothetical 1960 convention which we visit in your play, are political battles with real drama, real excitement, real suspense. What has happened to the political convention? Today, you wonder: how could they have not known who was going to be the candidate?

A. In 1940 there was an elaborate plot that no one knew about. Well, some people knew about it—those who were in on it. I was a kid, and even though I lived in the house of a Senator, he wasn't included in it, he was a Democratic senator.

France had fallen, I think it was around May 1940, and the conventions are around June or July, and England is endangered by Hitler, and Roosevelt and the Eastern establishment, which governs the Republican party and has great control over the Democrats—the banks and the corporations wanted us to go to war against Hitler on the side of England. It was a virtuous thing to do at one level, but against the will of the American people. Before Pearl Harbor, which was the next year, '41, 80 per cent of the American people did not want to go back to a war in Europe. We'd been stung in 1917 with the First World War, we got nothing out of it, except prohibition of alcohol which made us a lawless country. So here they are, trying to get us into the army again to get us to fight in Europe, but the country is isolationist. One of the reasons why the word has been demonized is because they had to do it. The average American is an isolationist.

Q. That is one of the most striking things about the picture you paint of America in 1940: Today we are told about "the greatest generation" that went and fought Hitler, but you remind us just how powerful the sentiment was in 1940 against going to war, and how hard it was for FDR to change public opinion.

A. That was the case. The country was isolationist, as it has always been when left alone, and not hyped, as it were, by the media, which in turn are owned by international banking systems interested in making money out of war. The people did not want to go, there wasn't anything FDR could do to get us there. He did everything he could to help England. He did the destroyers deal and we got some bases out of it. Come 1940, he makes the historic decision that he will secretly help England, and that he will run for a third term, which no President had ever done. And his Republican operators would see to it that the Republicans also nominate someone dedicated to getting the United States into a war on England's side against Hitler.

And that's what I begin the book with—that is what that 1940 Republican convention was about. They had picked a Wall Street lawyer with a strong Hoosier accent—Wendell Wilkie, "the barefoot boy from Wall Street" he was called. They decided they were going to nominate him. Now, the convention wanted to nominate Robert A. Taft, the leading conservative in the county, and a noble, if somewhat limited figure, but he certainly would have kept us out of the war if he had become President. So they had to destroy Taft. Well, they did it—read the book to see how they did it, but it was an astonishing story.

I was there, in the audience with Senator Gore, my grandfather. From the age of ten he was blind, and this is one of the reasons why I was prematurely overeducated in politics, because I read to him. He wanted to go to that Republican convention, even though he was a Democratic senator. So we went there and sat in the gallery and we watched Wendell Wilkie being created by this extraordinary cabal, which involved the Cowles bothers, who owned something called *Look* magazine, I think Henry Luce was involved in it, and they defeated the isolationists.

And the galleries—they were bringing in people from the streets, I think they were paying some of them, and they would start this chant, which would go "We Want Wilkie! We Want Wilkie!" It was an extraordinary crescendo of sound, and after a number of ballots, they got Wilkie.

Now Roosevelt was covered. Should he die—and he always knew that he was going to die in office, he was not a well man—or, if he were defeated, then the next Republican president, Wilkie, would support his foreign policy. That was my first encounter with conventions. It seemed open, and it seemed democratic, and of course we learned later that is was beautifully manipulated.

The next convention I went to was the Democratic convention in 1960.

Q. You were a candidate in 1960.

A. I was a candidate for Congress from upstate New York, and I was also a delegate to the convention which met in Los Angeles, which picked Jack Kennedy over Lyndon Johnson. That was fairly fixed in advance, but there was room for maneuver. Johnson was quite prepared to use, if he could figure out how to do it, the fact that Jack Kennedy probably wouldn't have lived much longer. He suffered from Addison's Disease...

Q. Which we didn't know. You might have known, but none of the rest of us knew in 1960.

A. I knew, and the family knew, and Johnson knew. I mean, everything is known among a certain group that has to know things. Jack was known as "yellow Jack" in Congress.

Q. That's what you called him in the book.

A. He was bright yellow, and he said it was due to malaria, and indeed he had had malaria. But it was also part of having no adrenal function. He would turn this awful color. Later he looked like he had a permanent suntan, that was the way they sort of modified the color of his skin. So Jack was in danger from that threat from Johnson, but Johnson didn't dare hit. I don't know why, but they scared him off. He came by the New York delegation to work us over and said, "I had a heart attack a couple of years ago, but I'm in perfect shape now. I said 'Bird,[6] you better cancel that blue suit I just ordered' [to wear in his coffin]. And Bird said, 'You're going to be fine.' I said, 'well, one way or the other I'll be wearing it'" [i.e. alive or dead].

Now that was not only a nice joke, it was a cryptic remark about Jack's health. Those of us in the delegation knew what he was doing, but everyone else was mystified. It just didn't make any sense at all. Here's a young man, he's not going to die of anything.

A year before that, in '59, I wrote this play, *The Best Man*, in which the Democratic Party was divided. On the one hand, we had Adlai Stevenson loyalists—Stevenson had been our

GORE VIDAL TALKS POLITICS

candidate in '52 and '56, and Mrs. Roosevelt, his chief supporter, wanted him again in 1960, and a hard core still did, right till the end. But the Jack Kennedy insurgency had happened, and a lot of Stevenson-ites were defecting to Kennedy.

I remember when Arthur Schlesinger finally went over to Jack from Stevenson—he didn't know Jack at all in those days. I remember Mrs. Thomas K. Finletter saying, "This is the greatest betrayal since Benedict Arnold." Feelings were high. Adlai Stevenson was still being pushed by Eleanor Roosevelt. So Jack Kennedy talked to Frank Roosevelt Jr., and me, and Walter Reuther, who was the head of the United Auto Workers, and also the intellectual of the labor movement and the great favorite of Eleanor Roosevelt, suggesting that the three of us go up to Val-Kill cottage, where she lived at Hyde Park, and talk her into supporting him.

Q. That was a big job!

A. She gave us dinner, and she had a position paper which turned out to be her next day's "My Day" column on why Stevenson should run, why Stevenson should be elected. And Frank Jr. said, "Now look, Ma, he won't say he's running. He's been asked all week, and he won't say." She said, "Well, that's the way he is." And Frank said, "Well, yes Ma, that's the way he is, and that's why we don't want him." Anyway, we didn't budge her, and she didn't budge us. Then the convention came.

Q. This is when Gene McCarthy, Democratic of Minnesota, made his famous speech nominating Stevenson, "do not neglect this man of honor…"

A. Yes, it was a great speech, but she gave a speech first. And she came out without a note. She was extraordinary. She was a very, very tall woman, and she just dominated the convention hall. She said, "How dare you turn your back on this man, who has led this party, and all that we stand for, the New Deal, and all. You want to turn your back on this man, who, even though he lost twice, got the most votes any Democrat had ever got before." She balled out the delegates, and they just sat there like kids. She waved her finger at them. She really put on quite a show.

Then the Catholic Eugene McCarthy goes up. I give his religion because Kennedy was Catholic, and a lot of people, particularly in my upstate district, voted anti-Catholic. I would have been elected to Congress had Kennedy not been on the ticket. There was an anti-Catholic rage that went through the Hudson Valley. He didn't do well. So Gene McCarthy was and is a rather serious, thoughtful man, and sort of in the German Catholic tradition which is very serious stuff. He thought Jack a flippant figure of no depth.

Q. There was good reason to think that in 1960.

A. There was good reason to think that until the end. I was charmed and delighted by Kennedy personally, and certainly he was intelligent. But any man who gave us an invasion of Cuba, a missile crisis, and the war in Vietnam in 1,000 days—give him another 1,000 days, and we would be irradiated atoms in space. No, he was a mistake as president.

This is all the background to the play *The Best Man*. I gave the manuscript to Jack to read, and he gave me a couple of very good lines, and he did say, "You know, we don't spend a lot of time talking about the meaning of it all." I said, "Jack, you've been running for four years, I've only got two hours in the theater, I've got to concentrate it to move it along." And he said it would be the first play he would see after he won the election. And it was the first play he saw after he won the election.

Q. So what would have happened in 1960 if the convention had listened to Eleanor? Stevenson would have been nominated. He might not have won, but Gore Vidal would have been elected to Congress from the Hudson River Valley. What then would have become of Gore Vidal? Would you have worked your way up and ended up in White House and not given us twenty-three novels?

A. No, I would have never gotten to the White House because I wrote *The City and The Pillar*. And that eliminated me. In *The Best Man* I put in a problem something like that, a smear I was using against my two rival candidates in the play. I would have been limited to the House, and maybe to the Senate and that would have been it.

Q. Would you have been happy in the Senate?

A. Oh, in the sixties, yes. As a Senator in the eighties, when I ran again, really just to show the flag—

Q. In '82 you ran for the Senate in California—

A. —in the Democratic Primary. Really I ran just to show the flag and to say certain things that the other candidates were not talking about. You force them to talk about it. The *L. A. Times* is very good about that. If you bring up a subject that the other candidates won't address—like the military budget—they then ask all the other candidates, and they've got to comment on it. As an educational exercise it was fun—educational for me as well.

But Senator Cranston, who was a Senator from California at that time, explained it to me. He said, "You know, you're elected for a six-year term. If you want to be elected for another six years, you must raise $10,000 every week of your six-year term." I had enough money of my own to keep me going during the campaign, but in trying to raise money, they give you a list of donors, and you have to call up a perfect stranger and ask them for money. The first thing I discovered during that race was that I am constitutionally incapable of doing that.

Q. So you would have had a short career as a senator.

A. I would have had no career, but I wouldn't have wanted one once I realized this was the condition. You're not going to be a statesman of any sort; you're going to be a mendicant. You go to fundraisers, and that's all you do.

Q. It's hard to imagine Gore Vidal pleading for money from the corporate bigwigs.

A. I remember I did talk to one. I'm not entirely pure. At Fluor,[7] they had a little money for a possible liberal, just as a garnish as it were. And I talked this guy a couple of times. We both decided that I would be no use to them in the Senate.

Q. That's probably true.

A. Probably true.

Q. Let's go back to 1960 for a minute. In 1959 you write *The Best Man*. There is a question of casting: who was going to play the Stevensonian hero of the play—idealistic, but vacillating? Who was considered for this part?

A. It was a hard part to cast, because most middle-aged actors who are right for a presidential role are essentially American boys who got just old. Because movies stars are boys, and female stars are girls, and they start out as boys and girls, and they start out playing boy and girl, and they keep on playing boys and girls, and they generally have no transition into a more mature presence. So I was faced with a lot of fifty- to sixty-year-old guys who are still playing high school seniors from Pomona High.

They don't sound right, they don't sound like intellectuals. Franchot Tone was going to do it, and then his health was peculiar, so he didn't. And then suddenly MCA said, "How would you like Ronald Reagan?

Q. Ronald Reagan?

A. Ronald Reagan. He had fallen on hard times. I think that year was the year that he did a nightclub act in Las Vegas, reading jokes off a teleprompter or whatever they had in those days, and introducing showgirls. And I said, "Well, he is a very good actor," which he is. This business about him being a grade-B actor is nonsense, nonsense put out by the Republicans, because they thought it might occur to people that he is brilliantly acting the part of a President. He doesn't know how to do it, but he knows how to act it—which was indeed the case. He's a wonderful actor, but he is Pomona High School. He's got the high school boy voice, and I don't think he would be convincing to an audience as an Adlai Stevenson-type of candidate. So I am forever known as rejecting Ronald Reagan as not being a credible President to a theater audience. We cast Melvyn Douglas instead, who went on to greater stardom.

Q. Now, let's just speculate again: what if you had accepted MCA's offer and cast Ronald Reagan as the lead in *The Best Man*?

A. He would have had a renewed career, as Melvyn Douglas had, after he was put in it. He would have been a star on Broadway, something he never did, although he was used to speaking on platforms. Or my fear about him not being very credible as an intellectual might have sunk the play. I think I made the right decision, though the great joke is being rejected as a presidential candidate by me for Broadway, he then had to become governor of California, and on to the White House.

Q. Whereas if you had just given him a chance, he might have made a career on Broadway, and had a long and happy life in the theater.

A. Except I think he always would have ended up in politics. He was obsessed by politics. However, the door didn't open for him until he became the spokesperson for General Electric. He introduced that TV program, and then he made thousands of speeches for them on the virtues of capitalism and the horrors of communism—which is essentially the campaign speech that he gave all his life. So, if he had the G.E. Theater, I think he would have become President in any case. If he had the lead in *The Best Man*, like Spalding Gray currently, and Melvyn Douglas originally—

Q. And Henry Fonda in the movie—

A. Henry Fonda in the movie, he would have had a renewed career.

Q. I want to go back to *The Golden Age*, your new novel about history. I'm speaking now as a native of St. Paul, Minnesota, and I wanted to say how much I appreciated your taking the reader to visit St. Paul in 1940 to meet the boy wonder Harold Stassen, Governor of Minnesota. It's also where you introduce us to Wendell Wilkie. How did you get the brilliant idea of shifting the scene to St. Paul?

A. Because that's where the scene shifted. Because that is where Wendell Wilkie made his first heartland speech. Gardner Coles—that was his real first name, wasn't it?

Q. Yes.

A. His nickname was Mike Coles. The Coles brothers published a very successful picture magazine called *Look*.

Q. And they published the *Minneapolis Tribune*.

A. Yes. So they thought they would start him off in St. Paul, to see how he took with the audiences. He couldn't give a written speech, but he was great at improvising. So they have coverage for radio, and they have newsreels and so on. But he makes a terrible speech, and Wilkie throws away the pages of the script and says, "Well, that's over with," and he walks up and down and improvises, and the house just explodes. They realize they've got a viable candidate here, and so he speaks across the country. And they are manipulating the Gallup polls, manipulating all the polls, making him look more popular than he is, making it look like people are more eager to come into the war on England's side, though they never got a good polling answer on that one. I describe his entry into Philadelphia, I've got his hotel—you know, these details are all correct. If I say he was at room such and such at the Blackstone hotel in Chicago, or whatever it was, he was there.

Q. So you actually did a lot of archival research. This actually happened in St. Paul?

A. Oh yes. In St. Paul, I have Governor Stassen come there to introduce him, and he's got two state troopers with him, and they all have a ghastly dinner at a diner before he goes on stage. That's pretty much what Stassen said and did. T.W. Lamont, the head of the House of Morgan, was in town to look over the new Republican internationalistic candidate. I followed the facts very, very carefully.

Q. Your play *The Best Man*, which opened in 1960, has some uncanny contemporary notes, although do I understand correctly that you haven't changed a single word from the original script?

A. Yes, this is the original script.

Q. One of the biggest lines for the audience last night, I noted: a political person says: "In those days, you had to pour God over everything like ketchup." The audience in the theater burst into laughter, obviously remembering just a couple weeks ago, when Joe Lieberman referred to God seventeen times in his acceptance speech.[8]

A. It's come back. We didn't do God much in the sixties.

Q. What do you make of the presence of God in the political field today?

A. I deplore it, naturally. After all, I am an atheist, and if people want to promote these cults they should do it not through the political system but through the social system. If people want to go to church, they have every right under out constitution to do it. It's about tact. And I think that is where the Senator from Connecticut lost me. It's tactless to lay your religion upon other people. It makes it sound like you have found the golden way and no one else has. That is impertinent, and rather dangerous, in a country as sectarian as the United States, in a country with so much religious bigotry boiling around under the surface.

Q. Americans go to church a lot more, they tell us, than Italians.

A. Oh, Italians don't go near churches, unless it's to get married. But I don't believe those statistics about the heartland, or "the chigger belt," as H.L. Mencken called it—

Q. Oh dear.

A. —where the Gores come from. Mississippi. Yes, there's a lot of church-going, because there isn't much else to do in those villages. Social life revolves around the church. As Eudora Welty said to me, "There isn't really anything else to do up in the north of Mississippi, where the Gores come from. Of course, I'm from the city. I'm from Jackson. We're not quite that religious down here." But no, religion is back. Only 20 per cent of the American people accept evolution, accept Darwin. Now, if America is supposed to be keeping abreast of the civilized world, I would say we are already falling pretty far behind. We have the worst educational system for the average citizen, for the non-rich, in the world. The history textbooks—you know about them. Frances Fitzgerald wrote brilliantly about them.[9]

Q. Yes she did.

A. Then we invented something called terrorism. Only two American planes have ever been damaged by terrorism—one was at Lockerbie and one was out of Athens.[10] Neither took off in the United States. For those two airplanes, we are totally harassed by the American government. The American citizen is asked, "Did someone else pack your bag for you? Did you leave your bags anywhere at any time? Do you have an ID with a photograph on it? Well, no that won't do!" I have to carry a passport in my own country. Now this really reminds you that you are in a police state. This is like traveling in the Soviet Union twenty years ago. I find this intolerable, and I don't know why people put up with it. The only terrorism against us is provoked when we blow up an aspirin factory in Sudan.[11] And I think the Sudanese have been very nice not to blow us up with a kamikaze bomb or something. We have been overactive and over-provocative everywhere, and the American people have not been told about it, because obviously the media belongs to the provokers. We are kept in innocence and we are kept in ignorance, and this is not healthy.

Q. I want to talk about third party politics in this country a little bit. Your new book *The Golden Age* has quite a sympathetic picture of Henry Wallace's 1948 run for the presidency, and you have yourself have been both a Democratic candidate and part of a third party effort after 1968. How do you evaluate the Nader campaign this year[12], and how does it compare to Wallace in 1948, which started out as sort of a good effort and then ended up very weak and disappointing.

A. Nader waited too long. He could have been more active. I suggested running him in the early 60s, when he was first getting known. I did a big piece about him and we put him on the cover of *Esquire*. I said, why not have a President who has done a few things, besides running for things, and he has done the following things that would be useful for the American people. Seat belts may not be very dramatic, but at least he did something useful.

He took on big business and the auto industry. I was told he wasn't very pleased with my piece.

I've never met him. I was interested in him four years ago [1996], and then of course he did nothing. He just said he was a candidate, and they put his name on the ballot, and that was it. He's working harder now. But you're not going to build anything around him. People say, oh it gives the Green Party a position on the ballot, which means they'll get federal funding four years from now. Four years from now there may not be an election. Everything has just ground to a halt. The second law of thermo-dynamics is working beautifully, entropy is up ahead. Nothing is working in this country. Representative government has stopped.

There isn't one person in America who has ever thought about politics who doesn't know that every single member of Congress is paid for by corporate America and it isn't to represent the people of their state, it is to represent corporate America's inter-ests, which are not those of the people at large. So, they've given up on the idea of having representatives in Congress. They see two candidates this year [Gore and Bush] who, whatever their pluses or minuses, represent nothing at all that has to do with the people. These are people who go to fundraisers, who create fundraisers. Bush became the Republican candidate because he has the same name as a failed President, and he got 70 million dollars on the strength of that from corporate America. Gore is running neck and neck with him. So, that system is over.

First of all, we shouldn't talk about a third party or fourth party—we should talk about a second party. I mean, we've got one party, the party of corporate America, with two right wings: Republican and Democrat. There are ways of creating political identity and interest in the country, but you'd have to go to that, 60 per cent, I would guess, that don't vote—at least not in congressional elections, and well over 50 in presidential elections. I'm sure this year 60 per cent will not vote for President. I would go out there and start looking among those people. They aren't stupid. They aren't well informed, how could they be? They don't believe the newspapers or television, but they know things are wrong, and why somebody—a billionaire with some sense of civic duty—doesn't go out and—I mean, only 14 per cent of America people are unionized, but I'm sure there are some workers who wouldn't mind having better healthcare, and better retirement and this and that, that are quite discontented with the way things are.

You would begin, as it were, by "beating the Bushes," looking for the majority, because it is a small minority that votes. One per cent owns the country, as we know, and their political operators deliver the government to them each time, which means the treasury, which means dividing it up. Presently, 51 per cent of the budget goes to the military. That's going up because the Pentagon is getting restive, giving ultimatums to the Clinton administration, as they will to the Gore administration. They will get the payoffs they want—and there isn't any money for anything else.

Q. Al Gore says the central contest today is between the people and the powerful.

A. I must say, the road to Damascus is more crowded than I thought. We are, the Gore family, probably the principal populist family of the south. It goes back to my grandfather, and my great-grandfather, his father, who was a Civil War veteran, to the 1880s when the Party of the People was founded. It started in Georgia, South Carolina, but Mississippi was a great catalyst, because in northern Mississippi they weren't slave owners, they were rednecks, and they were Unionists. They were against the Civil War, they only went out of patriotism to their own class.

But the Party of the People was an exciting movement. It was made up of farmers who had been ruined, and they got in workers from the north. They put together a very vibrant party, whose off-and-on official voice was William Jennings Bryan. Now the East, when they saw this, knew it was dangerous. A party of the people—and they called themselves that—Populists. You know more about this than I do because I haven't written about it yet. But the co-opting that went on, and I know this from my grandfather, he organized Oklahoma as a state—previously it was Indian territories—and he brought them in to the Union in 1907, he was their first Senator. By then, the Populists had become Democrats or Republicans, generally Democrats. So he had been a Populist candidate in Texarkana, Texas in 1896, but by 1907 there was no question of running as a Populist in the new state of Oklahoma or the state of Mississippi. It had been co-opted by the Democrats.

Then came the fatal union between the banks—eastern banks—as represented by Woodrow Wilson, and the Populist forces as represented by William Jennings Bryan. The payoff being Bryan becomes Secretary of State under Wilson. My grandfather in the Senate was the Populist leader, along with Lafollette, who was the Progressive leader from the North. So this uneasy balance, FDR forged into the greatest political machine we'd ever seen. For about twenty years it governed the county, uneasily. What did the former slaves and former slave holders have in common with bankers from New England? But with FDR they all got along for a time.

Q. There was a fascinating piece in the *New Yorker* by Nick Lehmann, who has been writing profiles of Gore and Bush. He says, "Let's look at the fathers of today's candidates in the thirties."Albert Gore Sr., the Senator, was from one of the poorest parts of America in the thirties, where everyone went broke, while at the same time, George Herbert Walker Bush, future President, was being driven by his family chauffeur to his prep school. Class differences were immense in the thirties. But they are not so different for the sons today.

A. I think Albert Jr. has moved out of—what was it, "ten cent cotton"? [a very low price for cotton farmers] "Ten cent cotton" was one word to us. It meant poverty. I grew up with that. My grandfather, Chairman of the Agriculture Committee, said that every year the head of the Grange would come in front of his committee and said, "Senator, I've got to tell you: the crop has been below average for the last eighteen years." No, the South didn't rise till the second World War, and the fact is that they kept their Senators and Representatives in Congress forever and they became chairmen of committees, so the South is sinking under the weight of these military bases.

Q. But our Al Gore didn't grow up with ten cent cotton.

A. No, Albert Gore Sr. had freed himself of that world, though he represented "the folks" in Eastern Tennessee, which was always the liberal part of Tennessee. Albert Jr. was brought up in Washington, D.C. I remember them going on about the Fairfax Hotel, a luxurious hotel where they lived for nothing, because our grandfather Grady Gore owned it. He was very colorful.

When George Washington came along, inventing Washington, D.C., he conned these Maryland farmers who owned what is now the District of Columbia. And my direct ancestor, a Gore—Thomas Notley Gore, I think it was, owned a big farm which contained what is now the White House, and all the way up what they called the Tiber River up to Capitol Hill. We sold out and went west, which in those days meant Mississippi. There was one Gore who stayed and is rich as Croesus today, and Grady built this small hotel, the Fairfax, and gave Albert Sr. and Albert Jr. shelter for many years. It was a kind of seedy boarding house. It's called the Ritz Carlton now, so everybody thinks it was always grand. It was not.

Grady always financed Senator McKellar, who was a horrible old man from Tennessee.[13] Now Grady tried to get McKellar on the phone, but McKellar wouldn't answer his call. Grady got so angry he called up Albert Sr. and said, "I've got $20,000 in cash here and I was going to give it to McKellar but I can't get him on the phone. I'm going to give it to you and I want you to beat him." And that is how Congressman Albert Gore Sr. became Senator Albert Gore Sr.

Q. George W. Bush, Governor of Texas: his main claim to fame seems to be, as you pointed out, that his father was President. But where in the world do sons succeed their fathers as heads of state? Syria, Jordan, and North Korea come to mind. Isn't this un-American?

A. It has happened before. The Adams family, who are the most distinguished family ever in American politics, even more than the Roosevelts. Father and son, or father and grandson, both held office. Forget the Bush family, they are the most negligible family in the country. They are unintelligent, they are reasonably decorative, they are obedient to the great economic powers. Nixon said something interesting to Murray Kempton about Bush senior when he became President. Murray and Nixon used to have lunch, and when Murray said, "Well, what is this Bush like?" Nixon said, "Oh, nothing, nothing there, just a lightweight. He's the sort of person you appoint to things, like the U.N., the CIA. But that Barbara Bush, she's really something; she's really vindictive!"—which was the highest complement that Nixon could deliver.

Q. The one thing we have not talked about in your book, *The Golden Age*, is the most striking part of it: your detailed picture of what FDR did to convince Americans to overcome their deep-seated isolationism and agree to go to war against Hitler.

A. It was an elaborate plot. First he made sure the Republicans would nominate somebody who would be an interventionist in case he died or got defeated. So with Wilkie he felt safe. He and Wilkie were then plotting, that he would serve out his fourth term—he was elected in '44. Roosevelt would have his fourth term, and then, if still alive, he would not run for a fifth term, but he would run Wilkie. And they would form a new party—the liberal end of the Democrats, the liberal end of the Republicans, and specifically the interventionists—because now we have created an empire. We were masters of Europe, Western Europe, and we were the masters of Japan. We had everything, and we should have an imperial party to go with it. Which would also be a Wall Street party, with some interest in the people, as Roosevelt's New Deal had done more for the people at large, things like Social Security, than any of his predecessors.

However, Roosevelt dies not long after his fourth inauguration, Wilkie dies, and Truman inherits. So Roosevelt's plan had fallen to pieces, because he wanted to live in friendship with Stalin, and he recognizes Stalin's sphere of influence, and Stalin's paranoia, and Stalin recognizes that we were in charge of the entire Western hemisphere. We were now in charge of the Pacific ocean and we are now in charge of Japan, we were really in charge of everything. So why not get along with Russia, who will take at least two or three generations to catch up with us, and by then of course it's a different world.

The machinations start in the beginning of *The Golden Age*, and my sort-of heroine, Caroline Sanford....

Q. I like Caroline.

A. Oh, she's a good character. She was in *Empire*, and she was in *Hollywood*. In fact, I've described her in those novels ever since she was a young girl at the turn of the century. She'd gone to the same school that Eleanor Roosevelt had gone to in France, but later. So, she just comes to Washington and is invited to stay at the White House, as they casually did with a lot of friends. I'm able to use her inside as a pair of eyes, and she has sort of a flirtation with Harry Hopkins, who I knew pretty well, since my father worked with him in the Roosevelt administration. Hopkins is one of the most fascinating figures in our history. I show the details as they unfold chronologically.

Then you see him goading the Japanese into attacking us. Finally, I think it was in August of 1941, he delivers an ultimatum that they must get out of China. Now they've been trying to conquer China since 1937. And here we are blithely telling them they must get out of China, or we will turn off the oil, which we did do, and they are dependent on American oil for their war machine. And we stopped all sale of scrap metal. They have no metal; they have to buy scrap from us. With that, they had to attack us. Roosevelt knew it. And if they attacked us, then Germany and Italy would come together, as they had an alliance with Japan, and with luck, would declare war on us. That was exactly what happened. The wickedness of Roosevelt, of course, was Pearl Harbor.

Q. Do you think Roosevelt knew that Pearl Harbor was going to be the target of this attack?

A. I read everything that was available, and there is a lot of stuff that became available as of 1995, because of the Freedom of Information Act. Yes, I think he did know it. Circumstantial evidence says that he did. In fact it was Charles A. Beard who wrote the first book on the steps that Roosevelt had taken to get the Japanese to attack us. The White House line was always that yes, they knew there would be an attack, there would be a rupture after our ultimatum, but they thought they would attack Manila, as that was nearby. However, we were reading all of their codes. They had something like sixteen naval codes, and we had been reading them. We knew where their fleet was, and the fleet was saying, "We are going to rendezvous near Wake Island," and so on. They were over in the central Pacific, and the only thing below them was Hawaii.

Another cousin of mine, Admiral James O. Richardson, Commander of the Fleet, was relieved of duty when he fought with Roosevelt at this point. He said, "You've got to send the fleet back to San Diego." That's where the fleet was stationed. He said,

"They are overexposed in Pearl Harbor, there is no motive for having them at Pearl Harbor." Roosevelt said, "They are staying." Richardson, in his memoirs, said he told the President, "If you want a war, what you're doing is provocative, and may bring one on. You should realize that the senior officers of the navy do not have confidence in this administration."[14]

He was relieved of his command then and there. He was a great friend of my grandfather's, as well as his cousin, so I had picked up a lot of that stuff during his lifetime. I have no proof, no smoking gun. But a week before Pearl Harbor, Franklin Roosevelt wrote a letter to his new friend, Wendell Wilkie, and said, "We may be attacked before Monday."

That letter exists. But the court historians are never going to bring any of this out. I don't know how they gloss it over. I've had my battles with them, as you know, with the Lincoln Brigade. The way they ignore evidence is a startling thing, and I think they should be in religion rather than history.

Q. Gore Vidal, thanks so much for talking to us today.

A. Thank you.

4

Radical History Review Interview
Ravello, Italy
July 12, 1988

The Radical History Review *was edited by a collective of two dozen younger historians, many of whom were Marxists and/or feminists, some of whom have gone on to win Pulitzer Prizes and other top awards and win election to leadership positions in organizations including the American Historical Association. The* Review *was committed to analyzing the American empire, and from the beginning, in the late 1970s, it featured interviews with elders who had pioneered the critique of mainstream liberal history-writing. This interview was conducted on July 12, 1988, at Vidal's legendary home in Ravello, Italy.*

Q. In 1984 you told *The Washington Post*, "The American people have a passion to know about their past, but the TV networks won't show it because they've made up their minds that if Americans had a clear view of their past they might not like the present, might change it." Your critics call you a compulsive cynic, but this sounds very optimistic.[1]

A. I can say from personal experience that the popularity of these reflections of mine on American history in the form of novels proves that there is something going on out there. Apparently, the minority that reads books is very interested in the American past, and it beats me why the television networks, which are nothing if not greedy, don't plug into that. But they don't. I think the thing is much more complex. Partly it's that the educational system is now so bad. History is taught very badly.

Q. History is not a popular subject.

A. No. It comes in number 50, I think, out of 50 subjects in one of those "Purdue Polls" of high school students. But it's taught so badly. Is there any design to that? I'm not a conspiracy-type person, but I do think that there's probably some motive for making our history lethally dull. If you want, let's say, to deny the people certain rights, keep them ignorant of the Bill of Rights. If nobody understands who we were, we won't question why we are what we are. After all, if you had an educated electorate, you couldn't get away with forty years of a national security state, and you couldn't elect people like Reagan. So it's to the interest of the oligarchs— the national security statespersons—keep the people ignorant.

Q. Then you don't think that people are hopelessly hypnotized by the media or they're helpless in the face of advertising?

A. There are people and there are people. The people who see a Spielberg movie are still not a majority of the American people.[2]

People who read books are an even smaller minority. A book like *Lincoln* in hardcover was the number two bestseller of 1984. Number one is *Ludlum*. So I'm in competition with pop writing. There's nothing wrong with pop writing. I'd rather have people read a bad book than no book. At least there's hope they will go on to literature of some kind.

Q. The project of your book *Empire* is an unlikely one. If anyone else had gone to a publisher and said that he wanted to write a novel about the origins of American imperialism during the McKinley administration, he wouldn't have been given very much of an advance.

A. Perhaps not quite seven figures.

Q. Yet you were confident that this would be a bestseller.

A. No. It doesn't quite work like that. There is an audience for my books on American history; that audience is determined by their past performance. Seventy per cent of all books are sold by these great chains. It's all done on computers. You press my name in connection with an American historical novel and the computer estimates its probable sale—two, three hundred thousand hard cover, and then the Book-of-the-Month Club will take it. So bestseller status is sort of built in, even if I am doing "The Niece of Chester A. Arthur." The subject of the American empire was a rather good one for that time, which could not have been calculated by me or anybody.

Q. The book tells about the origins of the American empire in the Philippines and comes in the year that Marcos is in the headlines.

A. Yes, Marcos was in the headlines. But more important, the book came out right after we became a debtor nation. Thirty years ago I was the first person to bring into the discourse of journalism the phrase "the American Empire." In a review of one of my early books of essays, *Time* magazine did a raging attack on me, saying that one of the things that made me such an evil figure was that I used that phrase, "the American Empire." We cannot be an empire, of course. I remember Jack Javits[3] years ago saying "Gore, how on earth can you say 'American Empire?' We don't have an empire. We're a republic. We believe in freedom and democracy." Now, I hope "national security state," which I'm currently explicating, will catch on.

Q. In your book *1876* your characters discuss the place of truth in fiction and historical writing. "What we think to be history is nothing but fiction," one character says. Another disagrees: "I want to know, I always want to know what is true, if anyone knows it." Therefore, he concludes, history is better than fiction. His questioner says, "But how can we know what is true? Isn't everything that is recorded just one person's effort to make himself look best?"[4] Clearly, this is a discussion about your own writing.

A. I don't have a name for my books on American history. I don't like the phrase "historical novel" because it seems to cancel itself out even as one says it. I usually refer to them as just reflections on American history or narratives.

I use the phrase "agreed upon facts." That is all a historian can use, and this is why the pretensions of the history departments sometimes set my teeth on edge. They really think there is such a thing as "historical truth," if enough of them agree. Well, they agree on many absurd things and I brought up the subject in my second go-round on *Lincoln*.[5] During the sixties, many blacks decided that Lincoln was a honky. Obviously he did not want the two races living side-by-side. His desire for separatism led him to advocate the colonization of freed slaves outside the U.S. That was not a practical solution, but he clung to the notion of colonization as late as July, 1864.

In the age of Martin Luther King scholar-squirrels were obliged to make Abraham Lincoln a generous, wonderful, loving man, a man without a racist bone in his body, who knew that the two races would be divinely happy together. The truth? He comes out very strongly for colonizing blacks in his State of the Union address in December, 1862. He asks for money to buy land, for a piece of what was then called New Granada, which is now Nicaragua.

LaWanda Cox has made the case that he could never have been serious about it.[6] Other scholar-squirrels decide he dropped the notion because he had a vision of Martin Luther King, standing in the saint's own temple with this dream. Abraham Lincoln changed, they argue. Well, he didn't change, though the logistics of removing several million mostly unwilling people was, finally, beyond him.[7]

Now the squirrels are trying to eliminate the evidence that he never really gave up the idea. Ben Butler said that a few weeks before Lincoln died, Butler talked to him and Lincoln was still talking about colonization. One squirrel has determined that Ben Butler was not in town at the time, and that that eliminates Ben Butler as a witness. So they all agree that this conversation never took place. But it could have taken place a bit earlier. And Butler is writing many years later. They tend to overlook John Hay's letter of July 1, 1864. Hay said, he's "sloughed off that idea of colonization."

This sentence is acknowledged. Hay's next sentence is ignored: because of political thievery involving shipping, Lincoln has been "about converted" to the barbarousness of colonization. The "about converted" doesn't sound to me like a sprint to Damascus. Anyway, the history department revisionists are eliminating a witness to the Lincoln administration who is neither more nor less reliable than anybody else. Ben Butler's a liar. Hay is sloughed off. Now they can say Lincoln had given up on the idea of colonization two years before indeed he did.

I have the same problem with the *New York Times*. They have consistently lied about me, misinterpreted things that I have said in interviews, changed the wording around, right down to the preemptory strike they made against the dramatization of *Lincoln*. A week before it appeared on TV they got this hack to come in and say it isn't accurate. He gives a garbled report, to say the least. Now the *New York Times* is a primary source for any historian.

If you go through the clips, and there's a clip that says Abraham Lincoln gave an interview this morning and he said "I love the blacks and I want them to stay here forever, preferably in my wife's bedroom," there it is. In the *Times*. So what is history? As Tolstoy said, "History would be a very good thing if it were true."

Q. Could you talk a little bit about how you work? When you sit down to do *Lincoln* or *Empire*, do you take notes like the rest of us?

A. I'm not very good at notes. Oh yes, I'm indebted to scholar-squirrels. Were it not for them I couldn't do my work. I don't do very much primary source stuff, but neither do they unless they're focusing on some small area. I've got several thousand books downstairs, which is sort of a basic library. When I start on a book I just go around and get as many "texts" as I can find. I use different libraries when I'm back in the States. At the moment I'm doing 1917 to 1923. All those books over there in the corner, on those tables, there are about a hundred that I have to have at hand, biographies of Wilson, Theodore Roosevelt, Hearst. I'm also going to do a lot about the origins of Hollywood. It seemed to me that the real theme of *Empire* was the invention of "news" by Hearst. Now I'm going to show the invention of the world by the movies, a far greater theme than Warren Harding's administration and in a way rather more interesting than Wilson, though the Wilson era was a climacteric in our lives.

Q. Could you tell us about your formative political experiences?
What was the process by which you became a radical?

A. I don't know how I did. I was brought up in an extremely
conservative family.

   The British always want to know what class you belong to.
I was asked that on the BBC. I said "I belong to the highest
class there is: I'm a third generation celebrity. My grandfather,
father, and I have all been on the cover of *Time*. That's all there
is. You can't go any higher in America." The greatest influence
on me was my grandfather, Senator Thomas Pryor Gore. That's
his chair. Not from the Senate. From his office. He was blind
from the age of ten. He would plot in that chair. He made Wilson
president twice rocking away in that thing.

Q. He's denounced by Teddy Roosevelt in *Empire*.

A. Yes. T.R. didn't like anything about him. But T.P.G. was
only thirty-six, I think, when he came to the Senate. He was a
Populist who finally joined the Democratic Party. They all did.
He helped write the constitution of the state of Oklahoma, which
is the only socialist state constitution. He was school of Bryan:
anti-bank, anti-Eastern, anti-railroads, anti-war. Also anti-black
and anti-Jew—what they now call nativist. But he was not a crude
figure like Tom Watson or the sainted Huey[8]. He was a very literary man. So his prejudices were all low-keyed, except the hatred
of the rich and the banks—because farmers suffered at the hands

of capital that was in the East. They had no capital; only land and lousy crops. He was a tribune of those people. As he got older he got more and more conservative; later he wrote the oil depletion allowance. But he was honest personally. When he died, he was far from being a millionaire, which most Oklahoma senators are, with the exception of the sainted Fred Harris.[9]

Q. I gather you were not on the Left as a young man.

A. No. I was very much on the Right. I was a practical politician. This is very hard to describe, particularly in a journal like yours, where ideology and political thought matter. They don't care if you are brought up in a political family, with every intention of being a politician, which I had. There's no such thing as ideology. You have, as the Marxists would say, a structural response to things. You have class responses, which, as a kid, I was not about to start analyzing. But I thought of the world in practical terms. I knew how politics worked, which the theoreticians and the people who learn about politics in school never quite grasp. I knew that it didn't make any difference what your positions were, the game was power. I was, to use the boring word, pragmatic. That's how you get elected.

My first political activity: I was America First[10] at Exeter when I was fourteen. My guru in Washington was Alice Roosevelt Longworth,[11] who was a maniac on the subject. I knew a lot of the leading America Firsters. I did not see why we should go into a European war because I saw it in terms of the First World

War, and I still believe we should never have gone into that war, which my grandfather nobly opposed. Of course we didn't know anything about Hitler at the time—I'm speaking now of 1939 and 1940. In 1941 it all changed. The Japanese attacked us and I enlisted in the army at the age of seventeen as a private.

Q. What happened between your America First days at Exeter and your work on the national security state and the American empire in the 70s?

A. I suppose it was an evolution. In 1948 I wanted to go into politics and I was all set to establish residency in New Mexico, whose governor was a good friend of my grandfather's; I would have been put on the ballot as a presidential elector in the 1948 election, and, as I have an Hispanic name—although my family is from the Alps—plus the help of the governor and his machine, I was all set to start out and have a conventional political career. But I'd written *The City and the Pillar*, which described the life of a young man who was gay.

Now I must make a decision: am I going to publish this book and get into a lot of trouble, or, shall I suppress the book and go out to New Mexico and settle in Santa Fe and, in due course, go to the House and the Senate and whatever might happen. I made a decision. I think that is what we call a radicalizing decision.

Q. Then you would say sexual politics played a part in your radicalization?

A. It played a crucial part. You see, my first two books had been greatly admired; the *New York Times* thought I was wonderful.

Q. So you were not prepared for the response to *The City and the Pillar*.

A. I knew it was going to be rough. Luckily, being brought up in a public family I could handle that rather more easily, I think, than somebody who is shy.

Q. What do you mean, it was "rough?"

A. You must remember I was highly praised at nineteen and twenty for the first two books, particularly the first one [*Williwaw*]. That was one of the first war novels. There were four or five of us young war lions, and we were the toast of the country. Then I published *The City and the Pillar* and I hardly get a good review in the United States. I'm totally blacked out for my next five books by the *New York Times*. The daily reviewer said he would never read, much less review me again, and five books went unnoticed by him, by *Time*, by *Newsweek*. I had been demonized. Once you're a demon in our society you are ignored until you, somehow, become unavoidable. Then you are trivialized.

I had taken on the whole establishment of a pretty rustic country and said "Fuck you, you've got sex all wrong." Thus, I found my role. I exist to say, "No, that isn't the way it is," or "What you believe to be true is not true for the following reasons."

I am a master of the obvious. I mean, if there's a hole in the road, I will, viciously, outrageously, say there's a hole in the road and if you don't fill it in you'll break the axle of your car. One is not loved for being helpful. So my radicalization begins with *The City and the Pillar*.

When I was blacked out, I saw the powers of censorship in a free land and that made me a little cynical about freedom. I was told by Harvey Breit of the *New York Times*—a good friend of mine, he was number two at the book section—that "anything you publish will not be reviewed in the daily and you'll get a bad review on Sunday. Why don't you do something else or write under a pseudonym." So I did both. I wrote Edgar Box books in '52, published them over the next years.

Q. What is this?

A. Edgar Box: three mystery stories that were very successful, published in every language. One of them is out again in Italy this month. Rave reviews in the *New York Times*. Twenty years later I brought them out under my own name and the *Times* slammed them.

But that wasn't enough to live on. Then in 1954 *Messiah*, the best of my early books, came out; it was barely reviewed here. I was getting a fine press in England, and other countries, but nothing in freedom's land. So I went into television. Although the *New York Times* still didn't like me, they didn't take television very seriously and it doesn't make much difference whether you got a good review or not. From '54 to '64, I wrote television; I wrote movies; I had two hit plays back-to-back on Broadway, which is fairly rare. Lester Markel, who ran the Sunday section at the *Times*, was so affronted by the success of my play *The Best Man* that he called up four different writers to write an axe job. One of them was Richard Rovere; Murray Kempton was another, and finally, Douglass Cater wrote a tepid piece.[12] From '54 to '64 I made enough money for the rest of my life, which gave me an independence that the John Updike Chair of Quality Lit at Rutgers would not. In my busy decade I wrote, I think, a hundred television plays, about twelve movies, three Broadway plays, and started writing essays.

In my long, roundabout way, I'm answering your question. After *The City and the Pillar*, the next radicalizing thing was Joe McCarthy, watching the blacklist in operation. I wasn't directly affected because I almost never joined anything. I was also the wrong age to have been a Communist, and probably the wrong class as well. If I had been ten years older I might have been a Communist, but I wasn't. But I was horrified to see friends in television—writers, actors—not be allowed to work. With every play, the producer would have to submit every name of those involved to the network for approval. The process was inscrutable, more suitable to an Eastern Paradise than bravery's home.

I was deeply pissed off. So I decided that I would do an anti-McCarthy play on Philco-Goodyear Playhouse: something called "A Sense of Justice." The plot concerned a boss of a state played by E.G. Marshall. A young man decides to kill him out of a sense of justice. He's never met him, has nothing personal against him, but the young man sees him as a figure of great evil. He comes to kill him; and so on. It was very effective television. It caused quite a stir. Everyone got the McCarthy analogy. NBC was going to redo it the next summer; then—what else?—it was cancelled. So now we have two steps towards radicalization.

In 1960, I ran for Congress in upstate New York. By then I didn't have to worry about money anymore and it was partly a lark. A friend of mine, Kennedy, was running for President.

Q. You did a lot better than JFK in your district.

A. I ran 20,000 votes ahead of him, yes. And I carried every town. I carried Poughkeepsie, Kingston, Catskill, and Hudson. But the countryside made the difference in those days. The problem was Jack at the head of the ticket. If he hadn't been running, I would have been elected. That was old-fashioned politics. I quite enjoyed myself, but then I went back to novel-writing with *Julian*.

Q. You ran as a liberal Democrat?

A. I was the nominee of the Democratic and Liberal parties, yes. But there was no such thing as a real liberal Democrat. Jack was a very conservative politician, and I was much the same, as Al Lowenstein discovered. I think my campaign was the first he worked on. The 29th was the biggest district in the state. I had been working at it for five years before I ran. Judge Hawkins, the Democratic chairman of Duchess County, and I had put together a little organization. We had a hand in picking candidates here and there. There was not much in the way of liberal politics then. I wanted to clean up the Hudson River. I was premature with that. I also wanted recognition of Red China. Eleanor Roosevelt said, "For God's sake don't say that because there will be nothing but trouble from the China Lobby." I said "I don't think anybody will mind," and she said "At least say 'If they conform to the United Nations rules,'" so I used that dim formula.

I came up with the idea of the Peace Corps instead of military service. Of course it never occurred to me to ask what in the name of God we're doing with universal military conscription in peacetime. I hadn't thought that through. But I did think there should be alternatives to military service. So I came up with that idea and it was passed on to Jack by Harrison Williams, Senator from New Jersey. Jack then put it in a speech at San Francisco and that's how it got started. That was about all I did.

Q. Was there any gay-baiting in this campaign?

A. Even then it was considered bad karma to fuck around with old Gore. But just to be safe I had something on every politician and publisher in the district. There was one old newspaper publisher up in Columbia County, the most conservative of the five counties. He was making some giggly hints about me, and he was also having an affair with his son's wife. So after he took one particular swipe at me, I went on the radio in Hudson, the county seat, and I was asked, "Are you getting any ideas for any novels while you're doing this?" I said "Well, every now and then I do get an idea. I thought of a funny one the other day. A father and a son. The son marries this woman who's very good looking and the father has an affair with her." The whole county burst into laughter, and I never heard another word from the *Chatham Bee*, I think it was called. Do that sort of thing once or twice and you don't have to worry. In fact, the only real trouble I had was the *New York Times*. They ordinarily don't handle campaigns that far north. But they sent a special guy up to do an axe job on me for the Sunday section. It was too badly written to hurt, but it was the thought that touched me. Like the attack on *Lincoln*, the *Times* never sees a well that it doesn't want to poison.

In terms of radicalizing experiences, nothing much happened in that campaign except that I understood how the country worked politically. Also, by then favoring the recognition of Red China means I'm moving out of the pragmatic zone of politics. But I turned down a sure-thing election in '64 to go back to novel writing, with *Julian*, on the origins of Christianity. I've always been anti-Christian, but I wanted to know why. So I investigated the cult, a radicalizing thing to do since I come from that tradition. Then, from there to here, I don't know what happened.

Q. Your book *Washington, D.C.* ends up with a portrayal of a Kennedy-type figure as a ruthless and dishonest person.

A. Kennedy was just an operator. I was pro-Jack because he was a great charmer.

Q. What is the joke that you heard Kennedy telling about James Baldwin?

A. He called Jimmy Baldwin "Martin Luther Queen." He thought that was wildly funny. That's very Kennedy. The worst epithet that the Kennedys had for a man was that he's a "woman." Adlai Stevenson was worse—"an old woman." Except for Jack, I would say that that family, of that generation, anyway, had all the charm of two tons of condemned veal. You may use that.

Q. 1968 is the year of the New Left. It's also the year of *Myra Breckenridge*. The world is turned upside down briefly in 1968 and Myra is part of that.

A. Was. Now erased. Walter Clemons, my biographer, is going through that now, showing how carefully I'm erased from establishment versions of history. In the United States of America what ought not to exist does not exist. I am invisible.

Q. Myra in a way has the spirit of '68. She is wild, she breaks all the rules.

A. *Time* magazine wrote, "Has literary decency fallen so low?" The book was also the number one bestseller. So it's not as though it was obscure at the time. Of course it was also one of the greatest disasters ever made in the movies. It had more advance publicity than any movie since *Gone with the Wind*. Myra was on the cover of *Time*, of *Look*, of *Collier's*, all those magazines then. I've never seen such publicity. And then they made the world's worst movie, and the book was erased.

In '68, I connect up with the mainstream of the radical movement. I do three things in '68. One is *Myra*, which is sort of sending everybody up, including the sexual revolution, and I'm sending up the '60s types, too, because I'm not taking them too seriously. Then my debates with Buckley during the Democratic National Convention, which, of course, the whole country watches. Though I thought Mayor Daley and Abe Ribicoff more exciting.[13] Then I was caught in the Chicago police riot. The night Humphrey was nominated was the night that I was obliged to discipline Buckley. The next day, Marcus Raskin and Jules Feiffer and a bunch of us founded the New Party as a vehicle for Gene McCarthy. After we had gone to all the trouble to get the party's names on a couple of dozen state ballots, he torpedoed it. I just saw Marcus in Washington last March and he said, "You should have been our candidate." I said "I thought so too, but I was waiting for you to ask." He said, "Well, we didn't," and I said, "No, you didn't." We could have launched a real party at that moment.

With that I actually came out, as it were, into radical politics. Later I became co-chairman, with Ben Spock, of what later turned into the People's Party. I was involved '68 to '72.

I quit when McGovern, in the primaries, was saying everything we were, and rather better. That's when he wanted a law that $500,000 was the most you could inherit. Poor guy didn't know he was living in the wrong country. So there's the history of my becoming a radical.

Q. Your books of historical reflections are all about the unspoken fact that there's a ruling class in America.

A. Yep.

Q. How do you explain the ignorance of Americans about this elementary fact?

A. The Depression. Before that the ruling class was into conspicuous consumption; they built their palaces at Newport and they went with their diamond tiaras to the opening of the Met. Suddenly a lot of people are poor. But they [the ruling class] aren't poor. On the other hand, they're jittery. So they completely withdrew from the public gaze. A few went into politics, but it was frowned on. Of course they're all in politics, but they don't run for president; they buy the president. Nelson Rockefeller was considered a dangerous idiot by his class for turning the spotlight on them. By and large, since '33, they operate in the shadows.

Q. Your critics say these books are cynical.

A. They don't mean cynical, they mean realistic. But they have no way of knowing what the reality is. They are inoculated against the truth by the school system. They have been taught about all these saints—Washington, Lincoln, Jefferson—by the hagiographers who keep the saints polished and beautifully lit in the schools. And that's that. There are not now and never were any issues to agree or disagree upon. 1988. Why does nobody talk about the defense budget? Because the consensus requires that the money be wasted as it is being wasted. To point this out is to be cynical.

Q. Would it be fair to say that you're cynical about ordinary people in American history? The radical historians who came out of the '60s were very much interested in history "from the bottom up," portraying popular consciousness and popular experience; your radical history is very different. Some people have said what you find in Vidal is the portrayal of the masses as manipulated and deluded.

A. I don't characterize the masses because I have no conception of the masses. I don't know what the word means. I can understand administrative numbers, but that's something else. I write about the rulers because they leave records. The only members of the lower orders that keep diaries that I am aware of are lone, crazed killers of presidents. They always keep diaries. I don't know of any novelist of rank who does, but from Sirhan Sirhan to the guy who shot George Wallace, they all keep diaries.

Q. In *Empire*, you have Teddy Roosevelt worrying about the possibility of revolution if reforms are not made in the way that the new rich conduct their business. Ordinary people are a presence in the background of your central characters.

A. Madison's "iron law of oligarchy" is eternally true. From Shay's Rebellion on, the people have had the potentiality to disturb the reigning oligarchs. But nothing more. The American oligarchy has never not been in full control.

Q. Richard Poirer reviewed *Empire* in the *New York Review*; he said that while Vidal writes about the ruling groups in his historical reflections, you find out what Vidal thinks about ordinary people in his wild novels *Myra*, *Myron*, and *Duluth*.[14] There, ordinary people are portrayed as—

A. Off the wall. I think that's well observed.

Q. So you have put these two together to get a complete portrayal of American consciousness.

A. There was a very good critic in England in the '60s and '70s called Peter Conrad. He had a wonderful line. He was reviewing *Myron* and said people have been writing about how *Myron* is the sequel to *Myra* and they don't like it because of that, or they do, or whatever. He said it's not the sequel to *Myra*, it's the sequel to *Burr*. That's pretty shrewd. What I had done straight in *Burr*,

I'm now doing fantastically in *Myron*. After all, there is Richard Nixon wondering back in 1948 if they have extradition to his own period, whether he can stay there in the past or not, whether he will be pardoned. All of that is not unlike Burr on the lam.

Q. What Poirer seemed to be saying was that in your writing the ruling elites are extremely articulate and historically conscious, but the ordinary people like Myra live in a world of media images and are therefore totally deluded. That seems wrong. Myra is an extremely sharp person. Myra knows what's going on. Myra tells the truth.

A. I'll say. She certainly was onto overpopulation. Holy Myra Malthus, as I used to call her. On the other hand, if you want a version of the American as TV-watcher/consumer, *Duluth* tells it all.

Q. Your portrayal of Lincoln is different from your portrayal of everybody else in your historical books.

A. I don't go inside of his mind for one thing. He's only observed by others. That's a necessary cop-out. Shakespeare could have gone inside his mind, but I'm not Shakespeare. I wouldn't dare try.

Q. You leave readers in the same position as the people around Lincoln, trying to figure him out.

A. You can add him up any way you like in the book.

Q. At one level your critique of Lincoln is devastating. Basically you trace the national security state back to him: the suspension of habeas corpus, universal military service, high military budgets.

A. Certainly he left us with a centralized "blood and steel" state. And he had absolutely no right to hold the South in the Union. The South had every moral and constitutional right to leave. If Lincoln had taken his stand on the high moral ground of abolition of slavery, then he could at least have said, "There is a higher moral good than the Constitution." But he didn't. He took his stand on the Constitution and he fell right through the fabric.

Q. This is somewhat more interesting than the date on which Lincoln ceased to advocate the colonization of slaves.

A. Of course. This is the essence of *Lincoln*. I repeat all the arguments that he gave for the Union, and I have all the arguments that were made against him; his answers don't add up.

Q. It's a devastating portrait. You said subsequently that Lincoln demonstrated how, if you had sufficient will, you could manipulate the Constitution any way you wanted.

A. Sufficient will and a "military necessity."

Q. You said *Lincoln* provides a blueprint on how to subvert the country, how to rule by decree.

A. Exactly. Why do you think all the right-wingers have been reading the book and studying it?

Q. Yet your Lincoln is not an evil figure. He's a hero, a person with real authority. That kind of figure doesn't exist anywhere else in these books.

A. No. I think that maybe Washington was a bit like him, but Washington was always tangential to what I was doing. I was more interested in Jefferson and Hamilton. No, Lincoln was an autocrat. He was dictator. He was more benign than not, but God knows what he set in train.

Q. Yet you make him an admirable person.

A. Dictators can be admirable people, it's the fact of the dictatorship we don't like. We might like the man.

Q. Is there any explanation of Lincoln's motivation in your book?

A. Sure. It's all in that speech about ambition that he gave at the Young Men's Lyceum in 1837. In my first Lincoln exchange in the *New York Review*, I quote from the speech at great length.[15]

He predicts himself, he predicts Abraham Lincoln. He says that the ambitious man can not follow in another's footsteps. He must always be first. He cannot succeed to the office of the presidency that's been invented. He must reinvent it. He warns you against himself and then he goes right out and does what he says this man of the race of the eagle and the lion would do.

Q. In his review of the book, Harold Bloom wrote, "Lincoln's obsessive drive to preserve and restore the union was a grand restitution or compensation for what could never be healed in his own personal and familial life."[16]

A. I'm surprised Bloom would have latched onto that because I'm not a very personal writer. I don't put personal things at the center of people's characters. I'm convinced Lincoln did have syphilis and I'm convinced that Mary Todd died of paresis, contracted from him. I don't make much of it in the book because there isn't that much evidence. I don't think that anything he did was ruled by anything in his private life. Long before he had syphilis or was married, he had this urge to be great. It came from reading Shakespeare, it came from reading the *King James Bible*. That famous style of his also came from Blackstone. His favorite book was Parson Weems' *Life of Washington*. But, by and large, he didn't read history, he didn't read biographies, but he certainly had an idea of what greatness was: greatness was to be a founder.

Q. Lincoln is fascinating also because he is not a part of the ruling circles; he's a Westerner.

A. Yes. He's quite innocent of all that, although as a smooth railroad lawyer he could have become a Clark Clifford.[17]

Q. In the book you don't let us forget that.

A. Never for one minute. He had moved out of his class and by marrying Mary Todd he was announcing to the world that he was going to move into the aristocracy. Which, indeed, she was.

Q. One thing is missing from *Lincoln*: the Union under Lincoln undertook the most radical of all slave emancipations. Nowhere else was there such a massive war to destroy slavery, nowhere else were slave owners denied compensation, nowhere else were ex-slaves armed and enlisted in a war to abolish slavery. This doesn't seem to add up with the picture of Lincoln that you give us.

A. No. Because I don't believe it. A lot of things happen. A politician must do many, many things simultaneously and many of them are contradictory and this drives history professors crazy. But in the real world of politics you say one thing to John, you say another thing to George; they're perfectly contradictory, but it all comes out your way if you're lucky. The principal reason for an Emancipation Proclamation was that England was getting close to recognizing the South. If they did that they would be buying southern cotton and the South would be economically viable. That had to be stopped. Pressure was being brought on Lincoln to emancipate because there were a lot of powerful abolitionists in England. That's really what it was for.

Then he comes up with a proclamation emancipating not the slaves in the border states, that were still with the Union, but only the slaves in the South over whom he had no power. A horse-laugh went up in Parliament. American historians like to ignore that: emancipation was treated as a great joke.

The arming of black troops? Of course. They would try anything. But by and large he wanted to colonize the freed slaves and I don't think he ever let go of the idea. He finally gave it up because it was simply impractical. Nobody had the money, nobody had the ships, and the blacks didn't want to go. So that was the end of that plan. And that is the real Lincoln. The fact that at the end of war slavery was over—well, slavery was going to be over anyway, and he was in no hurry about it.

Q. In all of your historical books you tell the story of what happened through conversation. You portray our rulers as highly articulate, historically conscious people.

A. They used to be.

Q. Does this require that you distort the way things really happen? Do you portray them as more conscious and more articulate than they really were?

A. Let me say between "distort" and "distill" there can be a certain leap. Of course, I have to distill. Professional politicians never tell you anything and they certainly don't tell each other anything. They talk in code. I remember Jack Kennedy when he saw *The Best Man*. It was the first play he saw after he was elected. He loved it. I watched him from back stage just to see what was holding his attention. "The only overall flaw," he said— this is Jack Kennedy, drama critic—"is that politicians never, in my experience, philosophize about what they are doing." I said, "I've been around politics, yes, it's all in code." And he said, "Yes, you send signals." You can have a conversation which will swing a whole state and you haven't said more than four words. You just mention George, and you mention Tom; well, you know, the judgeship; yes, I know. That's all you have to say and somebody's going to get a judgeship and you're going to get the state. So I have to play Corneille or Racine to my native folk. Obviously I have to heighten it and distill it.

But whenever I have Theodore Roosevelt say something, other than "good morning," I've taken it from a letter or from a conversation. I'm not making up. The same thing with Lincoln. It's all stuff he's been known to have said or something very like it. It's just that you don't do as much of it in real life as you have to do in fiction, where you have to concentrate it.

Q. Tom Carson wrote in the *Village Voice*, "Vidal turns history into something made by enormously well spoken people." This sort of personifying of historical forces, he argues, leaves out a sense of a system which has its own requirements, its own dynamics. He says, "Who, reading his version of Teddy Roosevelt, could believe that Teddy was acting on behalf of any interest more abstract than his own crackling energy?"[18]

A. I think that's the only principle that he was acting upon. He had political debts to pay. He belonged to a political faction which he manipulated and sold out whenever it served him. With *Empire* I think that Mr. Carson is on fragile ground. They were extremely literary, this group. Teddy Roosevelt must have written twenty books. Henry James did say the things I have him say, Henry Adams said the things I have him say. You are talking about the most articulate generation that we've ever had. And Washington was, as Henry James says, the city of conversation. It was that way right up through my own youth. Everybody talked, and talked quite well.

Q. You write about history in different genres. You write essays as well as novels. Before *Empire*, you wrote a long essay in the *New York Review* on Teddy Roosevelt where you dealt with the same issues as the book. And you have the wild books like *Myra*. How do you decide which genre is appropriate to which issues? Why not a wild sex farce about Teddy Roosevelt and a sober and scrupulously accurate assessment of gender in twentieth-century America?

A. I would have to have the genius of Doctorow.

Q. On the Jewish question, your article "The Empire Lovers Strike Back" in *The Nation* offended many people.[19] Podhoretz says to Vidal, "To me the Civil War is as remote and as irrelevant as the War of the Roses." Vidal writes, "I realized then that he was not planning to become an 'assimilated American,' rather, his first loyalty would always be to Israel."

A. Let's look it up. What I wrote is always shaded this way and that way in order to change the meaning. It's been so shaded now that I am supposed to have said that all Jews are Fifth Columnists. Now here's the exact sentence: "'Well, to me,' said Poddy, 'the Civil War is as remote and irrelevant as the War of the Roses.' I realized then that he was not planning to become an 'assimilated American,' to use the old fashioned terminology, but, rather, his first loyalty would always be to Israel. Yet he admits that they ought to remain among us in order to make propaganda to raise money for Israel, a country they don't seem eager to live in. Jewish joke circa 1900: a Zionist is a someone who wants to ship other people off to Palestine."

I had this out with my old friend Norman Lear, who said, "You can't say assimilated." I said, "Come on, you started People for the American Way. Well, which are you? If you're not going to be an 'assimilated' American, then what are you? Are you an Israeli who happens to be living here?"

My argument is only weak at one point: what on earth does Vidal care about nationality? I hate the nation-state. What am I doing saying you've got to be either a good American or a good

Israeli, but you can't be both? Why not to hell with both of them? That would demolish my argument.

But no Jew can do that, at least none who likes Israel, because they have to protect this peculiar little state. So, instead of hitting me where I am really weak, they get hung up and try to talk about anti-Semitism. Which has nothing to do with it.

Q. But you're also talking here about a historical consciousness of the American past, which is increasingly rare.

A. That may have to do with my age and class and background, but you can't expect me not to be.

Q. American historians understand why the Civil War is the key to our history, but I suspect that most twentieth century immigrants—Italians or Poles, or more recently, Asian or Mexican immigrants—have the same feeling that the Civil War is as remote for them as the Wars of the Roses.

A. You're absolutely right. But look at the context of my essay: the Podhoretzes are giving out marks for Americanism. They write about me, "He doesn't like his country." That's the standard neocon line about all liberals. "Well, one thing is clear in all this muddle," writes Midge [Decter], adrift in her tautological sea, "Mr. Vidal does not like his country." They talk about me not liking my country, but they have no interest in the Civil War—or, I suspect, in the United States except as Israel's financier.

Q. When I read this I had a different complaint: I'm not sure that their first loyalty is to Israel. I think they are more ideologically consistent than that. If there was some change in Israeli politics, if Peace Now gained power, do you really think that Podhoretz and Decter would be out on the hustings campaigning for a treaty recognizing the Palestinians?

A. Murray Kempton said to me, "No, their first loyalty is not to Israel, you exaggerate, it's to making it." This was the only game in town that they could play.

Q. Do you accept Kempton's view?

A. I think there may be something in it, yes.

Q. Let's talk more about the '60s. Some historians have argued that if Kennedy had not been shot he would have ended the war in Vietnam and saved us from our terrible fate.

A. I don't believe it. Too many people have told me that he was all for going on. A few weeks before he died, he said to old Mr. Canham, the managing editor of the *Christian Science Monitor*, "After Cuba, I've got to go all the way with this one." Somebody, I think it was Frank Church, said that Albert Gore—the father—was also talking to him about how they were going to "stand tall," or however he would have put that in his own style.

He loved war and he had this sort of schoolboy attitude toward it. He loved counterinsurgency. I teased him once. He was sketching insignia for the Green Berets.

Q. You saw him sketching insignia for the Green Berets?

A. Yes. I said, "The last chief of state that I know of who designed military uniforms was Frederick the Great of Prussia." He didn't find that very funny. He liked war. I think he would have gone on and on. I think he probably would have got out before the other bums did, but for most of his second term we would have been fighting in Asia.

When he gave that inaugural address I was thrilled because I was as stupid as everybody else. I remember it was old Max Ascoli, whom we used to laugh at—he was married to a Rockefeller, Italian-Jewish intellectual, ex-liberal, and put out something called *Reporter* magazine. Arthur Schlesinger and I were praising this wonderful speech, and Max Ascoli said, "I haven't heard anything so dreadful since Mussolini." We thought, "sour old Max." I remember Arthur said, "And now we hear from Eisenhower's widow." When you read that speech today you realize that we're declaring war on the entire world. The national security state's voice had spoken.

I asked Jack once about the Defense Department. I didn't know anything about the national security state then, but I certainly knew that they took up a lot of money and I knew that

I was paying 90 percent income tax in those days. This is what Ronald Reagan and I had in common, we were both paying 90 percent tax. And if you're a writer—or even an actor—who knows if you're going to go on making money? But we were getting to keep an agent's commission on what we made. This is the late '50s. And it was all going for this military budget and we couldn't understand what it was all about. It was "The Russians are coming! The Russians are coming!"

I remember I was up at Hyannis Port with just Jack and Jackie and Chuck Spaulding. Jack said, "Oh, the Pentagon, there's no way of controlling it." He said, "A president, if he wanted to devote four years and do nothing else, he might penetrate it." He said, "I think McNamara's the best man for it and he understands that kind of thing," et cetera, et cetera. This is 1961-62. He just accepted it as something that was uncontrollable. Now it's even further institutionalized, with bigger and bigger budgets, and untouchable.

Q. Those who defend the national security state say "the Russians are coming," but now we have Glasnost. If it continues, it's going to make it harder and harder to convince people that the Russians are indeed coming. Does this mean we are in for a change?

A. The change in the works won't be due to anything so intelligent. It's going to come from the complete collapse of the economic system when the Japanese stop financing our deficits through their quarterly buying of treasury bonds. When that happens, we'll fold the empire fast. The next president will probably be in charge of that sad task.

It is my impression from the Moscow meeting, and I've been back a couple of times, that Gorbachev is unilaterally disarming. He hasn't got the money and that's that. He knows we don't dare attempt a first strike against him. He isn't going to do one against us. When we challenged him on Afghanistan, he said, "Okay, I'll get out." And he gets out. Eventually they'll abandon the Eastern buffer states. Too expensive. Too much trouble. Too much minority trouble at home.

That leaves the United States with a very large omelet on its not-so-innocent face, because we've demonized Russia since 1917 and seriously since '47 with the national security state. We have nothing else to hold the country together but "The Russians are coming!" It is my theory that every treaty that we will make with them now will be made in total bad faith. I bet that the CIA is going to report within the next year that the Russians are developing Star Wars in Nicaragua and we must immediately invade because we are now at terrible risk. The oligarchs lie constantly because that's the only way we know how to hold together the United States. I'm praying for a large economic collapse so that we then put our house in order. That's my Henry Clay solution.

Q. In your 1986 essay in *The Nation*, "A Requiem for the American Empire," you write about intellectuals: "At the dawn of the empire for a brief instant our professional writers tried to make a difference. Upton Sinclair and company attacked the excess of the ruling class." But no longer because "most of our writers are paid by universities, and it is not wise to be thought critical of a garrison state which spends so much money on so many campuses."[20] Do you really think that intellectuals had more of an adversary stance in the early twentieth century than they do today? Midge Decter would say no, it's today that the intellectuals are the most anti-American.

A. Midge's idea of intellectuals and mine are not quite the same. When I said "intellectual" I had in mind something rather larger than paid publicists. Russian writers, for instance, set the tone for their country and defined its prospects. American writers did that even down to Mark Twain, who generally was too frightened to speak out and lose popularity, but by God he spoke out on the acquisition of the Philippines. Those voices were heard. Henry James: he didn't do it publicly because he wasn't that kind of person, but his private letters on the Spanish-American War are violently anti-imperialist. Howells[21] was superb on the Haymarket Riot. His J'Accuse at that time was one of the most powerful statements ever made by an American writer. "In the first republic of its kind in the world four men have been executed for their political opinions." That was a powerful piece. And Howells was the smoothest of our professional literary men. Yes, their voices were heard and were to a degree heeded.

Today I don't notice anybody with a voluntary audience saying anything. I think that the general flatness of intellectual discourse comes from the academization of not just literature but of everything. History, politics, everything is academic, and academic is government, and government is ruling class. It's circular.

Q. Yet the neocons are constantly sounding the alarm that the universities have been taken over by the Left.

A. I don't know what they mean by that. Anybody who says there's a hole in the road is a communist? That's about their range. I don't find any Left in America. But, mind you, I don't find much of a Left anywhere. On the one hand you have nervous pragmatists like Gorbachev who are not ruled by ideology and superstition, who are trying to salvage something; on the other hand you have the mad, who are fighting some specter, whether it be Islam, or communism, or Jesus.

Q. Before the 1980 election you urged people not to vote for Carter. You said that Reagan's administration would not be any different from Carter's.[22] After eight years of Reagan, do you still think that was the right argument? It seems to me that Carter would have been a lesser evil on Central America, on the Sandinistas, on the Supreme Court, on the balance between social programs and military spending.

A. I had not put it together then, but I knew instinctively that there was no difference between the presidential candidates. Now I realize that each represents the national security state.

You might have gotten some different Supreme Court justices, but so what? Whizzer White was Jack Kennedy's invention. That is to his eternal demerit. Are you so sure that Carter wouldn't have sent the helicopters into Managua, to be shot down like the ones he sent to Iran? I think he was a hopeless selection of the Trilaterals, the short-lived phrase we used in those days—which is all a piece of the national security state. I don't think that there's essentially any difference. He was over-attentive to detail and couldn't make anything work. Reagan has no interest in detail and can't make anything work.

Q. The national security state is a concept that historians have not put in the textbooks yet. How would you sketch out its history?

A. As you pointed out, you can even find roots of it in Lincoln. But officially it began in 1947. Really it began as a determination at the end of World War II not to disarm and to continue high government spending. There were legitimate reasons for that—a fear of going back into the Depression. Nobody was afraid of the Russians. Their omnipotence is one of the great myths. I knew Washington in those days; nobody took them seriously. They were a bunch of clowns. Everybody knew that they had lost 20 million people, they had no technology to speak of, what industrial capacity they had had been knocked out, we had the atom bomb. And yet this scare campaign was put on.

For the purposes of teaching I would start with '47, when the National Security Council, CIA, etc. were invented. Then in

1950 the NSC was set in motion with NSC order #68, a blueprint for the state in which we still live, where 86 percent of the federal revenue goes for war, and the rest supports the largely irrelevant cosmetic government of Congress and Judiciary and the never-ending issues-less presidential elections. Ollie North gave the game away on TV. In effect, he told the Senate, the Chorus, "We are the government of the United States and what are you clowns doing getting in our way? Don't you know that you are nobody? We are the government. We're saving freedom. We're saving mankind. And here you are screwing us up." Ollie was my road to Damascus. I gazed into those tiny little dishonest eyes and saw America, with a "k" that the NSC-ers had inserted in place of our "c."

Q. At one point in your not-too-distant past you spoke of the period 1945-50 as a "Golden Age" in America.[23]

A. That was also the age of the national security state that ate them up, but we didn't know it. That's my final volume if I survive, when I sum up all these books in my own life. I'm going to zero in on what an extraordinary period that was in the arts and in the life of the country. But now, with later knowledge—I'll be writing about it from the point of view of today—little did we know as we danced on the rim of Vesuvius, that deep below us infernal forces were at work and we butterflies would all be turned to stone.

Q. So the sense that this was a golden age now is tarnished?

A. No, it's not tarnished. It was a golden age, but the blighting was going on in secret. You know, the first thing the CIA did when they got their first funds, around 1949 or '50, was to infiltrate the trade union movements of Italy, Germany, and France to keep them from going left—not communist, just left. Then we established a military and imperial apparatus all around the world which did not—and does not—conform to the constitution of the United States and its agreed-upon republic. This was done by Harry Truman and Acheson, working with senatorial geese like Arthur Vandenburg.[24]

Q. Many things in 1947-48 were not kept secret. The Loyalty Security Act, the beginning of the purges of reds. 1948 is the turning point, with the smashing of the Wallace campaign.

A. Yes, but we didn't—I didn't, anyway—understand it at the time. But Henry Wallace understood it all. Particularly, when he was smeared as a communist in the 1948 campaign because he was anti-imperial.

Q. You've written a lot recently about the decline of American empire. You told *Interview* magazine that you "hate to fall into a Braudelian Marxist determinism, but I do think that nations just run out energy."[25] You suggest there is some structural dynamic that no ruling class could alter. Could you explain a bit more about the dynamics of empires as you see them?

A. Other countries come along and they're not all in sync, each goes through phases. Look at what is probably the greatest society the world has ever created—China, the Middle Kingdom, which had a good 1500 years and a rather lousy 400 years. China will come back, as Confucius himself is coming back there.

Q. But this is sort of a way of letting our rulers off the hook. It isn't that our ruling class is completely inept and incompetent, it's just that they are part of a historical dynamic.

A. I would be a perfectly good Marxist on that: what they do won't make any difference. If the thing is expanding and the energy is burning along merrily, you can't do badly. You can be Abraham Lincoln and Thomas Jefferson rolled into one. If you're on a losing streak, then the country's gone. Jack Kennedy knew that. He was talking about great presidents once and he said, "The more I read and the more I think about this job, everything is contingent upon what you're faced with while you're in it." That's really why I think he liked war, because he knew perfectly well that war presidents got better press, more space in the history books. I'm afraid it's as crude as that.

Q. You never attended college. How did that happen?

A. I graduated from Exeter and you really don't need any more education after that unless you're going to be a brain surgeon. I had read Plato and I had read Milton. I had read Shakespeare.

I had had fair American history. And a lot of Latin. That's all you need. And very good English.

Q. Did you know Reagan in Hollywood?

A. Yes and no. I've been at functions with him a dozen times. Hollywood is a very small place; he was active in television and I was active in television. In '59, I was casting *The Best Man* and MCA offered us Reagan to play the good guy, an Adlai Stevenson sort of presidential candidate. I said I just didn't think that Reagan would be very convincing as a presidential candidate. Instead we hired Melvyn Douglas. As a result Douglas' career was totally revived, he won every prize in sight and was a star from then on to his death. Reagan by then had nothing, he was by that time a host on that TV program.

Q. So if Reagan had been cast in the lead of *The Best Man*—

A. Melvyn Douglas would have become President—a very good President. And Ron today would probably be touring in *Paint Your Wagon*.

Q. Do you have any thoughts on how history ought to be taught?

A. Yes. I'll tell you exactly how to do it. You start in the first grade and you teach every creation theory there is, from Big Bang to Garden of Eden, give 'em all. Kids love that. With as many audio-visual things as you want to, since they're television children. In the next eleven, twelve years you make history the spine to everything you teach. Everybody takes it. You give them simultaneously what's happening in China, what's happening in Europe, what's happening to the Incas, and so on. It's riveting stuff and kids will like it. There are audio-visual aids—I'm trying my best to be up to date here.

As you go along you will naturally teach science, as science starts to evolve. Those who are going to specialize in it will start drifting in that direction, but they will never lose base with the spine that runs straight up from the first grade to the twelfth. The famous difficulties over teaching sex: by the time they get into puberty, sex is part of history. You can teach that along with everything else. Everything is ancillary to history, history is the spine.

By the time they get to the present, or as close as you dare get to it without being partisan, they have had a good notion of what happened to the whole human race between the Big Bang and the moment that they're leaving school. At the end of it? I don't think anybody seventeen should leave school without knowing about the Roman Empire, knowing about Confucius. They've got to know these things. Foreign languages should be woven through. I'd prefer them to learn Japanese or Russian, or Chinese. Anyway, this kind of pan-history, or whatever word you want to use, is not that difficult to set up. It's just that there are not that many people capable of doing it. But once you do set it up, it should be a dream to teach and boring to no one.

Q. And what about American history? What should our students today know about the history of their own country? Radical historians have argued that they should know more than the acts of the great white men.

A. We're talking about up to seventeen. You're talking now about universities, I would think. What I hate is good citizenship history. That has wrecked every history book. Now we're getting "The Hispanics are warm and joyous and have brought such wonder into our lives," you know, and before them the Jews, and before them the blacks. And the women. I mean, cut it out! Teach the history of the place: what were the problems? You'll certainly have enough spare to explain black and Indian problems, and why women were not enfranchised, and how they got enfranchised. All these subjects should come up in a normal way, and I think it can be done without loading any dice, you just follow the track. Finally, you wouldn't get to American history until you're about fourteen or fifteen anyway because America is quite recent.

Q. The last chapter is the rise of the American Empire, the national security state and a very quick coda.

A. I don't think they'd let you teach that, but even if you stop with the Civil War, or the First World War, you've done all that you need to do. I'd rather have them know the history of China and Japan, because they're going to have to live with the Chinese and the Japanese.

POSTSCRIPT
Remembering Gore Vidal

Victor Navasky tells one of the most revealing stories about Gore Vidal, who died July 31, 2012 in Los Angeles at age eighty-six.[1] In 1986, Gore wrote an essay for *The Nation*'s 120th anniversary issue. Shortly after it was published, Victor was invited to lunch by the publisher of *Penthouse* magazine, Bob Guccione, at his East Side townhouse famous for its $200 million art collection. "We had barely consumed the *amuse gueules* when Bob asked me how much it cost to get Gore Vidal to write his essay," Victor recalled. "When I told him we had paid each contributor to that issue $25 and Gore got the same $25 that everyone else got, he almost choked on his Chateau Margaux and told me he had offered Vidal $50,000 to write an article for *Penthouse* and Vidal declined."

Gore, who had accepted Victor's invitation to join the magazine in 1981 as a contributing editor, published forty-one articles in *The Nation* at those rates. Some of his most memorable quotes appeared in *The Nation*: "We are the United States of Amnesia," he wrote in 2004. "We learn nothing because we remember nothing." In that same essay he called the US a place where "the withered Bill of Rights, like a dead trumpet vine, clings to our pseudo-Roman columns."

Gore loved to talk, and I interviewed him many times—in front of live audiences, on the radio, and for print—and in many places. The most memorable was at his legendary cliffside house in Ravello, on the Amalfi coast of Italy, where lots of people visited him. We arrived a few days after historian Eric Foner departed; he told me his daughter had played in Gore's famous swimming pool with the children of Susan Sarandon and Tim Robbins. Gore sent my wife to sit by the pool with Howard Austen, his lifelong partner—she had a wonderful time with Howard—while Gore talked about his life and work in the deep shadows of his downstairs study.

In that interview, for the *Radical History Review*, Gore described his campaign to introduce the term "American empire" into the political discourse—and, later, the concept of "the national security state"—both of which were firmly rejected at the time by establishment thinkers. Indeed much of his writing for *The Nation* was devoted to elucidating those two ideas—and empire was also the theme of his six-volume series of historical novels "Narratives of Empire," which included number one bestsellers *Burr* (1973) and *Lincoln* (1984).

In that interview he also talked about his transformation from right to left, his path to *The Nation*. In the beginning he had opposed US entry into WWII. "My radicalization begins in 1948 with *The City and the Pillar*," he said—one of the first American novels about a gay man—with the "rough" treatment it received in the *New York Times*. Next, he said, came the Hollywood blacklist—he was working in Hollywood, and although never a Party member, was "horrified" to see his friends banned from the industry. The third step came in 1968, when he published the wild sex farce *Myra Breckinridge*, debated Buckley on TV during the Democratic National Convention, and then helped found the antiwar New Party, and then the People's Party, which he co-chaired with Benjamin Spock from '68 to '72. Then in 1981 Victor invited him to become a contributing editor, and he promptly accepted.

His first article in *The Nation*, in 1981, was "Some Jews & the Gays," a caustic response to several anti-gay articles in *Commentary*, the conservative Jewish magazine edited by Norman Podhoretz. His first big cover story for *The Nation*, "Requiem for the American Empire," was published in 1986 as Gorbachev was beginning to reform the Soviet system. Gore proposed that the US and the USSR—he called them "the white race"—should unite to fight off the economic threat from "one billion grimly efficient Asiatics."

The Asiatics didn't complain, but two months later, some Jews did, after Gore wrote that Norman Podhoretz's "first loyalty would always be to Israel," and that he and his wife Midge Decter therefore constituted "an Israeli Fifth Column Division" inside the US.

Many of us took that as another satiric barb, but Podhoretz had his associate editor at *Commentary* write to thirty people on *The Nation* masthead who had Jewish-sounding names asking whether they had protested the magazine's publication of "the most blatantly anti-Semitic outburst in an American periodical since the Second World War." (Nobody on the masthead resigned.) Arthur Carter, the Wall Street figure who had recently become publisher of the magazine, told Victor that the head of the Anti-Defamation League had complained to him about Gore's piece. Carter replied, "What do you think we are? It's *The Nation*, not the Jewish Federation Newsletter." Victor called that "passing the Gore test."

Gore was glorious before live audiences. At the *L.A. Times* Book Festival at UCLA in 1987, Royce Hall was packed with two thousand of what can only be called "adoring fans." Onstage I asked him what he had said to Susan Sarandon and Tim Robbins when they asked him to be the godfather of their son. His answer: "Always a godfather; never a god." I concluded by noting that he had pretty much done it all—novels, essays, plays—and won every award; I asked, "What keeps you going? What gets you up in the morning?" He had a one-word answer: "rage."

In the late 1990s Gore named Christopher Hitchens as his official "successor, inheritor, dauphin or delfino." But after 9/11, when Hitchens came out in support of the Iraq war and quit *The Nation*, Gore withdrew the nomination. Hitchens came back in 2010 with a *Vanity Fair* column titled "Vidal Loco," going after Gore for his endorsement of the "9-11 Truth" cause—which indeed dismayed many of us. (Gore held the milder version— that the Bush administration had advance warning, but let the attacks happen—rather than the view that the towers were blown up from the inside on Bush's orders.)

One of Gore's memorable quotes had special meaning for me—it came in his unexpected appearance in the 2006 documentary *The U.S. vs. John Lennon*, based on a book I had written about Nixon's attempt to deport Lennon in 1972 because of his anti-war activism. "Lennon was a born enemy of those who govern the United States," Gore said with a twinkle in his eye. "He was everything they hated. He represented life, and is admirable; and Mr. Nixon and Mr. Bush represent death, and that is a bad thing."

Gore Vidal wrote as a citizen of the republic and a critic of the empire. We won't have another like him.

ACKNOWLEDGMENTS

Thanks to Colin Robinson for coming up with the idea for this book, along with the title. Jay Parini, Gore Vidal's literary executor, provided indispensable help. Laura Bolt did a superb job assisting with the editing.

At the *Los Angeles Times* Festival of Books, special thanks to Maret Orliss for inviting me to interview Gore onstage at Royce Hall. And thanks to Ann Binney for helping.

At the Los Angeles Institute for the Humanities, thanks to Steve Ross and Louise Steinman for inviting me to interview Gore. Thanks to Claud Zachary at the USC library special collections department for help with the audio of that event, and to Allison Engel for digging up the archives of the event.

At KPFK 90.7FM in Los Angeles, thanks to former general manager Mark Shubb and to Marc Cooper for launching the program which provided the pretext for my interviewing Gore, and thanks to Marc Torres of the Pacifica Radio Archives for technical assistance.

At the *Radical History Review*, thanks to issue editors Mike Wallace, Greg Nobles and Jon Schneer, and to managing editor Amy Ward. Special thanks to Bill Billingsley for research assistance on that piece.

Thanks to Katrina vanden Heuvel, editor of *The Nation*, for giving me the assignment of writing about Gore for TheNation.com after his death, for editing that piece, and for permission to reprint it here. Thanks also to Victor Navasky for his help writing that piece.

Finally, thanks to Judy Fiskin for coming on that 1987 trip to Ravello—it was unforgettable—and for coming to all the other events as well. Her enthusiasm and support for this project were indispensable.

NOTES

CHAPTER 1: Los Angles Times Festival of Books, 2007

1. "Aleut": an indigenous person from the Aleutian Islands of Alaska.
2. The Secretary of Defense at the time was Donald Rumsfeld.
3. Vidal's memory is wrong here: the piece was by Matt Tyrnauer: "America's Writing Forces," *Vanity Fair,* July 01, 2003.
4. George W. Bush enlisted in the Texas Air National Guard during the Vietnam War to avoid combat.
5. William Jennings Bryan: Populist leader from Nebraska starting in the 1890s; three-time candidate for president as a Democrat: 1896, 1900, 1908.
6. The Academy Award for Best Feature Documentary in 2007 was given to *An Inconvenient Truth*, about Al Gore's campaign against global warming.
7. John R. Bolton: Bush's ambassador to the UN, 2005-2006.
8. "Heck of a job, Brownie": Bush praising his head of FEMA, Michael Brown, after New Orleans was flooded following

Hurricane Katrina in 2005. Brown resigned in disgrace, widely regarded as disastrously incompetent.

9. Vidal and Buckley famously debated as commentators on the 1968 Democratic convention for ABC-TV. When Vidal described Buckley as a "crypto-Nazi," Buckley replied "Now listen, you queer. Stop calling me a crypto-Nazi, or I'll sock you in the goddamn face and you'll stay plastered."

CHAPTER 2: Los Angeles Institute for the Humanities, 2006

1. *With Honors*, 1994 film starring Joe Pesci and Brendan Fraser.

2. Paul Bowles, novelist best known for *The Sheltering Sky*.

3. Vidal's Massey lectures at Harvard were published as *Screening History* (Cambridge: Harvard University Press, 1994).

4. *The Doors*: 1991 film directed by Oliver Stone, starring Val Kilmer as Jim Morrison.

5. Gore Vidal's mother divorced his father in 1935 and married Hugh Auchincloss.

6. America First was the leading organization opposing US entry into World War II and one of the largest anti-war groups in American history. Founded in 1940, it closed after Pearl Harbor.

7. Norman Thomas: Socialist Party candidate for president; Burton K. Wheeler: US Senator from Montana, 1923-1947.

8. John Peurifoy: US Ambassador to Guatemala, 1953-54, during the CIA-sponsored coup that overthrew the elected government of Jacobo Arbenz.

9. Guatemala was the classic "banana republic," where the plantations of United Fruit grew bananas for the US market.

10. Carlos Castillo Armas, "president" of Guatemala put in power by the CIA, 1954-57, ruled as a dictator.

11. *Song of Bernadette*, a 1943 film starring Jennifer Jones as a 19th century French saint who saw visions of the Virgin Mary in Lourdes.

12. Richard Shickel, a member of the Humanities Institute—film critic and author of books on film.

13. Michael Lind, "He's Only the Fifth Worst," *Washington Post*, December 3, 2006.

14. Kitty Kelley wrote best-selling bios of celebrities that were unauthorized. Her book *The Family: The Real Story of the Bush Dynasty* was published in 2004.

15. The Governor Nelson A. Rockefeller Empire State Plaza in Albany, constructed between 1959 and 1976 at a cost of $2 billion, was widely criticized for its vast size—almost 100 acres of government buildings—its lavish architecture and its displacement of working class neighborhoods.

CHAPTER 3: 2000 Shadow Convention Radio Interview

1. People's Party: an anti-war party founded in 1971 which ran Dr. Spock for president in 1972.

2. William Inge: author of hit plays in the 1950s, notably *Picnic* in 1953.

3. Dawn Powell: novelist of the 1930s and 1940s, then forgotten; Vidal played a key role in reviving her work in the 1990s.

4. At the Yalta Conference, Feburary 1945, FDR and Churchill agreed with Stalin on the postwar structure of Europe—creating a Soviet sphere of influence in Eastern Europe and dividing Germany into four occupation zones, to be governed by the US, the USSR, the British and the French.

5. Charles Beard: one of the founders of the history profession in the US, an opponent of US entry into WWII. Vidal published a book of his own using Beard's phrase: *Perpetual War for Perpetual Peace: How We Got to Be So Hated* (New York: Nation Books, 2002).

6. "Bird": Lady Bird Johnson, wife of LBJ.

7. Fluor Corporation: an international engineering and construction company working for the military and the oil industry, based on Irvine, CA.

8. Joe Lieberman: Democratic Senator from Connecticut, was nominated as the Democrats' Vice-Presidential candidate in 2000.

9. Frances Fitzgerald, *America Revised* (New York: Vintage, 1980).

10. Vidal was speaking a year before 9/11.

11. Clinton had bombed a pharmaceutical factory in Khartoum after receiving erroneous intelligence that it was a terrorist bomb factory.

12. Vidal was speaking before election day in 2000.

13. Kenneth McKellar: US Senator from Tennesse, 1917-1953, a Democrat.

14. Richardson's letter is quoted in Gordon W. Prange, *At Dawn We Slept: The Untold Story of Pearl Harbor* (New York: Penguin Books, 1981), 39.

CHAPTER 4: Radical History Review Interview, 1988

1. *Washington Post*, July 4, 1984. This interview was published originally as "The Scholar Squirrels and the National Security State," *Radical History Review* 44 (Spring 1989), 108-37.

2. Spielberg had just made *The Color Purple*, based on the Alice Walker novel about African-American women in Depression America, and *Empire of the Sun*, based on J. G. Ballard's autobiographical novel set in China—two relatively highbrow films praised by critics.

3. Jacob Javits: Republican Senator from New York, 1957-81.

4. Gore Vidal, *1876: A Novel* (New York, 1976), 29-50.

5. "Vidal's 'Lincoln': An Exchange," *New York Review*, August 18, 1988, 66-69; reprinted in *Vidal, At Home: Essays 1982-1988* (New York, 1988), 288-300.

6. LaWanda Cox, *Lincoln and Black Freedom: A Study of Presidential Leadership* (Columbia, S.C.: University of South Carolina Press, 1981).

7. Recently Eric Foner made an irrefutable case for the view that Lincoln's views of slavery changed: *The Fiery Trial: Abraham Lincoln and American Slavery* (New York: Norton, 2010). The book won the Pulitzer Prize and many other awards.

8. Tom Watson, Populist racist congressman from Georgia in the 1890s: Huey P. Long, left-wing populist governor of Louisiana in the 1930s; considered a demagogue by many.

9. Fred Harris: Democratic Senator from Oklahoma from 1964-73; he ran in the Democratic presidential primaries in 1972 and 1976 on a platform emphasizing "economic democracy."

10. America First was the leading organization opposing US entry into World War II and one of the largest anti-war groups in American history. Founded in 1940, it closed after Pearl Harbor.

11. Alice Roosevelt Longworth: the daughter of Theodore Roosevelt, born in 1884, a powerful figure in Washington political and social circles and a famous wit.

12. Douglass Cater: an editor of *The Reporter* magazine, who covered Washington and national affairs.

13. At the convention, Connecticut Senator Abraham Ribicoff denounced "Gestapo tactics in the streets of Chicago," and the TV showed Chicago Mayor Daley shouting back, off-mike. Lip-readers analyzing the tape later reported Daley's response: "Fuck you, you Jew son of a bitch, you lousy motherfucker. Go home." Nancy Zaroulis and Gerald Sullivan, *Who Spoke up: American Protest Against the War in Vietnam 1963-75* (New York: 1985), 195-96.

14. Richard Poirer, "American Emperors," *New York Review*, September 24, 1987, 31-33.

15. "Letters," *New York Review*, April 28, 1988; reprinted in *Vidal, At Home*, 272-87.

16. Harold Bloom, 'The Central Man," *New York Review*, July 19, 1984, 5-7.

17. Clark Clifford: lawyer and longtime advisor to Democratic presidents from Truman to Johnson, for whom he served as Secretary of Defense.

18. Tom Carson, "His Country, Right or Wrong," *Village Voice*, October 6, 1987, 53-55.

19. Gore Vidal, 'The Empire Lovers Strike Back," *The Nation*, March 22, 1986, 350-53; reprinted in *Vidal, At Home*, 114-19.

20. Vidal, "Requiem for the American Empire," *The Nation*, Jan. 11, 1986, 19; reprinted in *Vidal, At Home*, 105-14.

21. William Dean Howells, 1837-1920, "the Dean of American Letters," author, critic, and editor of the *Atlantic Monthly*, was outraged by the Haymarket executions.

22. Vidal, 'The Real Two-Party System," in Vidal, *The Second American Revolution*, 244, 245.

23. Walter Clemons, "Gore Vidal's Chronicles of America," *Newsweek*, June 11, 1984, 74-79.

24. Arthur Vandenberg: US Senator from Michigan, 1928-35; opponent of the New Deal.

25. Andrew Kopkind, 'The Chore of Being Gore," *Interview*, June 1988, p. 62-64. Fernand Braudel was a French historian and one of the greatest, who developed the study of large-scale long-term structures of capitalism in history.

POSTSCRIPT

1. Published originally at TheNation.com, August 1, 2012: www.thenation.com/blog/169182/remembering-gore-vidal. Reprinted with permission.

PERMISSIONS

The author gratefully acknowledges the generosity of the Estate of Gore Vidal in making these interviews available for publication.

Jon Wiener, "The Scholar Squirrels and The National Security State: An Interview with Gore Vidal," in *Radical History Review*, Volume 44, no., pp. 108-137. Copyright, 1989, MARHO: The Radical Historians Organization, Inc. All rights reserved. Republished by permission of the copyright holder, and the present publisher, Duke University Press. www.dukeupress.edu

The postscript is reprinted with permission from the August 1, 2012 issue of The Nation.com. For subscription information, call 1-800-333-8536. Portions of each week's *Nation* magazine can be accessed at www.thenation.com.

Printed in the United States
by Baker & Taylor Publisher Services